Praise for THE BIG SQUEEZE

Tricia Moody set up a blog for executives across the globe to share ideas, and from their input as assembled ten ways to immediately improve bottom line performance. In *The Big Squeeze*, he has created a combination of entertainment and reference that talks with us, not at us."

ick Morley, Chairman, National Center for Manufacturing Science (NCMS)

This book provides 10 great innovative solutions of which at least 3-4 would be helpful in olving almost any procurement issue facing a company today. This is a great read for people oking for 10 proven ways that can lower the third party spend in your organization."

ill L. Knittle, Global Procurement Director, BP (formerly British Petroleum)

Trish Moody shows how individual people – with their own needs and wants – affect how a ompany tries to compete with traditional and global rivals. 'Follow the Money' was the advice f Deep Throat, the Watergate informant; it would be Moody's as well. Read this book if you ant to separate facts from fads to survive in the new global community."

om Slaight, Vice President, A.T. Kearney Procurement Solutions

A business book that's entertaining, offbeat, plus need-to-know. That's an unbeatable ombination. [Thisbook] is for anybody who wants to be a corporate hero. Author Patricia loody provides everything but a moneyback guarantee. And she'd be safe in doing that. *he Big Squeeze* is a big winner."

ack O'Connor, Publishing Director Emeritus, Purchasing Magazine

Patricia Moody presents a memorable story filled with powerful and proven approaches for ompanies to leverage their spend and generate cash to drive profits and growth. At Waste lanagement, our procurement team proved that supply management can turnaround a ompany and return it to profitability and growth."

avid P. Steiner, Chief Executive Officer, Waste Management, Inc.

A must read for every C level executive, and a must do for every supply management ractitioner. Moody has hit the proverbial nail on the head with this steamy business novel. t] will get distributed up, down, and across my organization. If there were a recipe book for ost management, this would be it. Ka-Ching!"

im Larson, Vice President Purchasing, Michael Foods, Inc.

You'll chuckle at the send up of corporate life in the opening chapters; you'll get your money's orth many times over in the second half: Several year's worth of supply management ideas to nplement, and from the leading practitioners in the field. Even seasoned experts will come way with at least one new idea."

obert W. "Doc" Hall, Editor-in-Chief, Target Magazine ssociation for Manufacturing Excellence

"A Lean Purchasing Tutorial, wrapped in a novel reflecting today's workplace, that provides the reader with a practical understanding of supply chain management."

Jack Healy, Director, Manufacturing Extension Partnership

"As usual with P. Moody's titles, *The Big Squeeze* adds IQ points to any manufacturing reader in purchasing/supply chain management. And no one else writing for the industry today comes close to her ability to recreate what it's like working in the 21st century in America (Yes, Paris Hilton is in there!) with humor—her definition of 'heijunka box' is to die for."

**Sherrie Ford, Chairman of the Board and Executive VP, Culture
Power Partners, Inc. (distribution transformers), and Principal, Change Partners, LLC**

"The real world doesn't unfold like bullet points in a consultant's Powerpoint slide. Patricia Moody's fictional portrayal of United Manufacturing lampoons many of the organizational, conceptual and human failings that scuttle many of today's operational improvement initiatives. Her strategic sourcing suggestions offer guidance to executives who want to attack, and elimi-nate, excess costs in the supply chain."

David Drickhamer, Editor-in-Chief, Material Handling Management

"Drawing on the collective brainpower of hundreds of executives via an internet blog, Tricia Moody has written a highly-entertaining book any business leader who wants to cut waste and drop money to the bottom line right now will find invaluable. Bravo!"

Dave Nelson, former Sr VP of Purchasing and member of the Board of Directors, Honda of America Mfg., VP Worldwide Supply Management, Deere, former President and Chairman of ISM (Institute for Supply Management), VP of Global Supply Management, Delphi

THE BIG SQUEEZE
Ten Ways to Cut Your Spend 10% *Right Now!*

Books by
Patricia Moody

The Incredible Payback:
Innovative Sourcing Solutions
That Deliver Extraordinary Results
with Dave Nelson, Jonathan R. Stegner

The Purchasing Machine:
How the Top Ten Companies Use
Best Practices to Manage Their Supply Chains
with Dave Nelson and Jonathan Stegner

The Technology Machine:
How Manufacturing Will Look in the Year 2020
with Richard E. Morley

The Perfect Engine:
How to Win in the New Demand Economy by
Building to Order with Fewer Resources
with Anand Sharma

The Kaizen Blitz:
Accelerating Breakthroughs in Productivity and Performance
with Anthony C. Laraia and Robert W. Hall

Powered by Honda:
Developing Excellence in the Global Enterprise
with Dave Nelson and Rick Mayo

Breakthrough Partnering:
Creating a Collective Enterprise Advantage

Leading Manufacturing Excellence:
A Guide to State-of-the-Art Manufacturing

THE BIG SQUEEZE

Ten Ways to Cut Your Spend 10% *Right Now!*

by

Patricia E. Moody, CMC

THE OAKLEA PRESS

RICHMOND, VIRGINIA

First Edition

ISBN 1-892538-45-8

If your bookseller does not have this book in stock,
it can be ordered directly from the publisher.
Contact us for information about discounts
on quantity purchases.

The Oaklea Press
6912 Three Chopt Road, Suite B
Richmond, Virginia 23226

Voice: 1-800-295-4066
Facsimile: 1-804-281-5686
Email: Info@OakleaPress.com

This book can be purchased online at
http://www.LeanTransformation.com

*Please Note: Chapters 1 through 10 of this book are fiction. Any resemblence to
anyone living or dead is purely coincidental. If you think you've been singled out, you
may suffer from paranoia, and should probably consult your psychopharmacologist.*

Cover designed by Stephen Brandt

Dedication

For Bomber—It's all your fault . . .

CONTENTS

Contents continued on next page . . .

Acknowledgments

Hundreds of industry and consulting volunteers and bloggers shared their valuable ideas and experience. For a full list of the guilty parties, see the Blog Files.

Also, Chris Loup, of the Purchasing Management Association of Boston (PMAB), raised her hand and encouraged this wild idea.

Rich Weissman, also of PMAB, started wheels turning.

Senator Howard Dean, the first Internet candidate, who proved that web power could build an idea.

Clients BP (formerly British Petroleum), Respironics and Waste Management offered quiet inspiration to get it right.

Thanks also to Sandra Smith of Rowley, Massachusetts, for her automotive expertise; Glenn Luckinbill; Maria A. McIntyre, EVP/COO of the Council of Supply Chain Management Professionals; my buddy Dave Nelson.

Introduction

Walk this way . . .
Supply management is important.
As important as manufacturing used to be.
But companies are slow to move this way.

It's about money.

Let me tell you a story.

Once upon a time, at the end of a bypass, surrounded by a few acres of yellow-painted parking lines filled with pickup trucks and mini-vans, stood a mill. We could call it a factory or a manufacturing site, but really it was a solid concrete bunker, not unlike the millions of brick mills that used to eat pounds of steel and resin and tiny fasteners, churn them through miles of digestive processes that changed the raw materials' basic DNA and spit out thousands of shipments of valuable consumer stuff—things we wear and drive and play with and talk into. Even what we eat is a product of some 20,000-square-foot bunker like this one.

But what happens when the parking lot empties and the bunker goes silent, when thousands of faster fingers in places around the globe with names like Szenshou, Bangalore and Kuala Lumpur learn to make their own stuff and ours, too? The mill workers who learned how to dissect Bill of Material explosions and how to measure supplier quality performance can't go back to farming for a living. And there's not enough work in the call centers. Might there be a better way?

Chapter 1
"Monday nothing . . . "

"Monday, nothing, Tuesday, nothing,"
—Tuli Kupferberg, from the 1965 Folkways album,
The Village Fugs

7:28 AM

"Get the ramp!"

"Get on board."

"Status meeting, now, in the conference room, move it!
All hands!"

Steve Morgan's head stretched out from his white-walled office and around the corner, sounding the alarm. Polished by years of emergency meetings and dressing down shivering subordinates, his voice summoned the buyers and planners of United Manufacturing to Monday Morning Status Meeting. Like a muezzin's call to midday prayer, his basso profundo penetrated cubicles where planners and buyers hunched over desperate calculations, spreadsheets, computer screens, faxes, and cell phones. The first shrill alarm of week four, one week left to close out the fiscal year, rattled coffee cups. Two minutes to show time. Grab your shortage lists, check in with the production leader, get it all down, all committed, all scheduled for just one more expedite job, priority shipmcnt. Time to make the quarter. Everything was a rush.

This was going to be a seven-day week in Materials Purchasing, starting with the first interrogation, and ending with a final exhausted Friday 8 PM report out.

13

"Brzezinski?"

"Here, sir!"

"Marino?"

"Yes, sir!"

"Griffiths?"

"Brendanne?"

"Gross?"

"Uh huh."

"Price?"

(Silence.)

"Price?"

"Uh, Price is indisposed, sir. Seems his trip out to Amalgamated Components went well and he's a little slow starting up this morning. I'll check the men's' room."

For Steve Morgan, it was going to be a very good day. Monday morning roll call energized this purchasing veteran—a fresh opportunity to bang heads, to lean on late suppliers, to deploy the troops. Morgan adjusted the silver and turquoise slider on his string tie, pushed back his chair and took the floor.

Everything about Steve Morgan was skinny. Even his teeth were thin, yellowed rectangles of coffee-stained porcelain. His Adam's apple protruded as he prepared to speak. From a great distance, assemblers would watch him lope down the main aisle and cackle about Ichabod Crane.

But it was his deeper-than-the-Marianna-Trench bass voice that earned him the most notoriety. Steve's phone voice had a polished resonance that he practiced daily. "Morgan here" was a vocal signature intended to stir the bowels of callers. A simple "I need it by . . . yesterday" moved paralyzed subordinates to frenzied activity. The Voice was a powerful weapon.

"People! Listen up! We're in week four of the last quarter of this fiscal year. The product line genius marketeers blew it again. The forecast said 60 percent Euro units, and we bought 60 percent Euro units, but the customers want

60 percent American. Get Amalgamated and Second Source Suppliers on the horn. We need their shipments by Friday. We've got the overtime crew lined up for assembly, and WE WILL MAKE THE QUARTER . . . or at least the new forecast."

Morgan punched out a short list of tasks.

"Marino, we'll need the parts breakdown . . . Brzezinski, get me the POs . . . " And to Brendanne, the lone female purchasing pro, a tribute to the waning power of Affirmative Action, "Go check for ECOs."

Ed Candyman, Morgan's senior staffer, waved a withered paw. Thirty years at United had worn the muscle out of his body, but he still knew the difference between an ordinary expedite, and a real get-on-the-planes-and-park-yourself-in-the-supplier's-lobby crisis. The quarter might be salvageable, but he had to know for sure.

"Excuse me, sir, but Engineering changed the final configuration, and yesterday's shipment from Amalgamated was short. We can only run 96 units. What do you want us to do?"

"Do? What do I expect you to do? What did you expect? Move it!" sputtered Steve. "We don't get credit for missed shipments or parts in transit. Grab the shuttle to the airport. You can catch the first flight to LaGuardia and connect through Pittsburgh or Cincinnati. I'll call Ames down at Amalgamated and tell him you'll be there at 7 AM sharp to bring back the short parts. Don't come back without them!"

Candyman had spent a lifetime jumping into just this sort of crisis. The ticket-counter clerks recognized his palsied end-of-quarter gait as he hustled through the line. "One round-trip to Waterloo, no bags, coach please, return tomorrow morning." His destination may have changed— one day Binghamton, today Waterloo—but the same urgency, the same nervous twitches, underscored Ed's attempts to make the gate, make the plane, make the quarter. "It's a wonder he's still upright," they thought as they

15

noted the beer paunch and his expeditor shoes. Thirty years beat the average survival rates for United Manufacturing purchasing, but Ed was a veteran whose aging instincts stood up well when speed failed him.

The flight to LaGuardia was uneventful. Candyman nodded off, lulled by the warmth of a strong summer sun through his 23A window seat, the only daylight he'd see this time of year. There was never enough time. His kids, Junior and Thatcher, were taller and quieter now; they retreated to their iPods whenever he tried to start up conversations—mostly "Yeah," and "Nope," and "See ya, Dad" before they scuttled back into their electronic dens.

Still, life at United Manufacturing had been good, at least until these last few months, when late shipments and quality problems disrupted every daily schedule. The guys in Production were getting impatient, and Purchasing was not such a fun place for heroes like Ed Candyman to slide through their preretirement years.

Candyman didn't know how much more his stomach could take. A sour surge of hot bile filled his mouth; his innards tied French braids around last night's extra-cheese pizza, two more points on a bad cholesterol count. Down below his belt a low rumble churned his gut. Candyman's head jerked upright, fully awake now. He clambered over two seats and rushed six rows down to the aft lavatory. Would Amalgamated have the parts ready and painted when he arrived? Could he get them on the plane? Would there be a rental car waiting in Waterloo? And did the hotel have its usual Monday night prime rib? Phew. Another close call. Ed buckled up and reached for his stomach pills as he settled in for the next leg of this all-day journey.

Back at United Manufacturing, buyers wrapped up their summaries for Morgan's midnight review. Someone had misforecast this quarter's requirements, but it didn't matter. Every minute counted. Steve had his minions jumping at both ends of the line. Incoming inspection awaited a fresh box of starter components for the 60 percent American product requirements; Quality was ready to waive inspection if a good sample proved 100 percent okay. Gross' best assemblers were on call, but it was going to be close. Last end-of-month rush was nothing compared to the end-of-quarter furies United visited on its battle-scarred suppliers—all 30,000 of them.

Wade Jackman, Jack for short, the veteran transportation expert down in Shipping, was working the phones, scheduling trucks that would complete the glorious cycle of industrial birth. Wade was a weightlifter, a two-time runner-up in the Mr. Universe contest. He liked to pump iron in his spare moments; he was rumored to have tossed a recalcitrant trucker off his dock. A Day-Glo bumper sticker, Jack's credo, stood out on his desk: "A healthy body is a ready body."

Jack's jaws worked overtime as he stuffed one more stick of Juicyfruit gum into his toned pink cheeks. During lunch breaks he played hearts with a friend, a "fra" from Cable Assembly, but when end-of-quarter rush rolled in— and these times seemed to be coming weekly—there were no midmorning breaks, and there was no time to work out. To maintain muscle tone, Jack strapped on seven-pound ankle weights. Hourly walks down to shipping and incoming inspection guaranteed a substitute workout. Jack knew he had magnificent glutes.

For the newbies in United's Purchasing department, Jackman was the one guy you wanted behind you. He knew all the good truckers by name, and he could always find the paperwork in time to hit the highway. Freight forwarders and custom brokers speed-dialed his cellphone number. Jack lived for the rush. It was a great life if you could survive it.

Satisfaction

By Wednesday of Week Four, the whole plant hummed with the rhythm of trucks cycling in and out, cell phones and pagers on full alert, even an hourly intercom blast heralding peak performance all around. Boxes of scarce parts secreted in Field Service lockers emerged to fill short-ages. Taxicabs commandeered as delivery trucks expedited parts from far and wide, for United's supply base included over 30,000 sources, the best and brightest that purchasing could hang on a 20-page contract. Morgan's ten-page shortage list, only one of five different editions—one from Purchasing, one from Production, one from Quality and two from Marketing—stretched and grew to 28 pages, then shrank again to a manageable 12 pages, or 856 items.

Morgan's record for shortages, a 1999 orgy of "pig in the python" massive troop deployments sent to expedite 1,257 critical SKUs from the 300 most troublesome suppliers, remained unbroken. In one day alone, Steve's frenzied planners pulled in 39 parts originally forecast for next year, 17 complete sets of obsolete motors to be broken down and reassembled to meet current requirements and 12 unmarked boxes of plastic injection-molded components from United's main competitor, Myco. The stockroom sanded off the original part numbers, stamped in United's six-digit code, touched them up with a dab of black paint, and presto! New parts, one less item on the hot list!

Despite Steve Morgan's dogmatic recalculation of safety stocks, replacement of EDI and faxed expedites with his beloved ERP behemoth, there were still plenty of opportunities for individual heroics. Miles to go before I sleep. Planes to catch, promises to keep.

By Thursday, the assembly lines had joined the happy chorus of plant voices stamping out a familiar shipping rhythm. Overtime and temporary part-time semi-permanent seasonal workers picked up the slack for The Regulars who headed back behind the stockroom to catch a few winks. It was comfy and warm back there. Morgan himself was rumored to have bedded down in a cardboard pile during one of his many all-nighters.

Jack's steady stream of small trucks, big trucks, taxicabs and personal drivers streamed off the Interstate and stacked up three deep as he took command of the loading areas, weighted ankles moving effortlessly between inbound and outbound traffic. By Friday, Jackman's hourly "Bucks Shipped" bulletins were broadcast over the internal TV monitors. Sometimes he persuaded customers to accept substitutes with a promise of future deliveries. The goal was no shipment left behind, no order unfulfilled, no backlogs, no IOUs, no laggards, no problems. From assembly lines and cells all around the plant, streams of completed units of all sizes and electrical flavors flowed into deeper rivers of forktrucks running the ready items down to packing centers, where metal strapping, wood pallets, styrofoam and shrink-wrap machines pounded out their happy beats—thump thump thwack, thump thump thwack.

"God, I love it so." Morgan tipped back his master chair and planted a size-14 alligator boot heel on the desk. Time to tally up the shipments—$9,000,000 and climbing, $32,000,000 to go! Morgan knew that 80 percent of the month's revenue budget shipped on Friday (and over the weekend) and 70 percent of the entire quarter shipped out in Week Four. It was a pattern he'd grown to love—regular as sex, but riskier.

Friday noontimes were private moments for the operations executive. He liked to re-review the orders shipped totals, fingering the final tally of dollars out the door. He would linger on customer names, and sometimes inch his hand toward the phone for one last security check, though usually he knew that was unnecessary. Morgan's well-trained team had the quarter well in hand—up tight, out of sight. "Big bucks shipped fast" became his mantra, and it looked like United was headed for another target-busting revenue record under his command. He sighed. "A glorious time to be in Operations. Heroic, record-setting, an all-around blast!"

Next, he highlighted the key metrics—line items shipped, customer orders filled, and most important, total dollars out the door. He penciled notes on white 3"x 5" index cards, re-straightened the turquoise slider on his string tie, hitched up his pants and punched the Ready Broadcast button on his video phone. It was time to rally the troops for one last push, only yards from the goal line.

They were so close, Morgan could smell it—the accumulated early morning dressing down of laggards, the careful mentoring of new hires, even a rather painful but impressive total ERP installation that he knew would be declared complete (or dead) long after his promotion—all of it now flowed together in one glorious maelstrom of success stories—"got the parts," "they've committed for delivery tomorrow," "we talked Engineering into the old flavor." A hundred promises kept, deals done.

Finger poised on the Start Group Broadcast button, it was time for him to let headquarters know this man's push to win the race had taken performance to unheard-of levels. He was going to miss United's Purchasing department, but after this record-busting quarter, Morgan knew he would be needed down at headquarters where a Senior VP slot waited. Yes, it was so close, he could feel it—a quieter life in a stock-endowed neighborhood guaranteed his just rewards for Morgan's brand of hard-charging, visionary leadership. It was only a matter of time.

Chapter 2
The Meeting: Oh yeah? A Sinking Feeling

Edward Joseph Deaux, "Mucho" to his friends, founder and senior partner of the focused and growing consultancy Strategic Tactics Inc. (STI), eased his BMW 750i onto the last stretch of Interstate 80, 12 miles or precisely 16 minutes of highway before United Manufacturing's exit. It had taken Deaux three decades to reach this particular exit, escaping the tenements of Salem, Massachusetts' Point District—six acres of triple-deckers and brick apartments housing the worker families, the human capital, of the Naumkeag, the world's largest cotton factory. Deaux's whole family had gone into the mills, except for the sixteen-year-old pregnant sister who married young and slipped away, the brother who died in Vietnam and another who succumbed in Park Square to a rumored drug overdose. His Dad's rotted lungs had collapsed under a quarter-century of Camels and cotton dust.

Deaux had hyperopia. While a normal mill worker's kid could only see the red stitches on a baseball at 15 feet, Eddie could see the stitches, the seams, and the Rawlings imprint at 25. As a teenager, the gift of far-sightedness made Ed a great outfielder whose reactions conveyed sharp, clear focus. Sometime during his eighth and last grade at St. Joseph's School, Ed thought he could make out a line straight up and away from The Point—through Catholic High, followed by a spotty business education degree and basketball at Lowell State, which landed him an entry-level Human Resources job at United Manufacturing. Although Ed had clearly not truly left the brick mills behind, HR became his jumping-off point, the legal tender which he traded for the next step, and the next,

21

and the next—each one guided by his hyperopia, his well-honed people skills and the unacknowledged but ever-present fear of slipping back to the tenement where the rest of Ed's family waited, proud but jealous.

Ed drove on, oblivious to the human landscape that streamed out behind his taillights. Sylvia, Deaux' on-board navigation system, gently reminded him, "Turn left , Edward," as the sedan purred down United's access road. It was, Ed observed, one of late summer's, or was it early fall's, flawless days. You could see forever, and the blueness of the skies, had he taken time to look up, would have singed retinas unaccustomed to natural light. Perfectly on time.

Deaux concluded his 7 AM cellphone call with the senior partners back in Boston. Billings were up. He chuckled. It was like on-line banking—punch in the right access codes, and out spit checks and STI receivables to power his next BMW, his kids' tuitions, the summer homes, and a few secretly risky real estate investments that pushed Deaux' happy buttons. The partners knew, ever since Deaux' engagement at United began, that this little beauty spot represented a big training opportunity, a sinkhole into which every United employee would tumble in a decade-long commitment to total culture change. STI's portfolio of strategically tactical training offerings extended from the mundane, "Getting to know The Toyota Production System," to the sublime, "Green Belt Advanced Quality Six Sigma Lean Product Design."

It was STI's strategic intent to culture change from the top down. All three hundred of United's busy top execs would fill the first training class. In seven-member teams—there was magic in the number seven, one element of which was calculated on the net present value of realizable cash flow for just one more team member—they would explore new problem-solving frameworks while they rubbed elbows with strangers from operating areas whose metrics and wardrobes held no interest for them.

STI's Master Leader teams offered top CFOs, for instance, the opportunity to lose themselves in rough Bill of Material hierarchies as they tumbled from finished assemblies down through endless tiers of subassemblies and components, all the way to the depths of raw materials and even base chemicals. Engineering VPs discovered the joy of cell design, takt time and level-load calculations. For Production and Purchasing execs, very few of whom had risen to executive ranks, the learning opportunities were endless. All the sophistication and power of stratospheric strategic thinking at its highest stunned these bottom-feeders and, after the initial paralysis and oxygen deprivation wore off, even engendered fresh wardrobe awareness. No white socks here. Team members from Production and Purchasing took to speaking slowly, sprinkling their reports with freshly minted vocabulary including "complexity," "optimization," "traction," and even "platform."

From morning pep rallies to vocabulary, tests and study groups, followed by miles of enterprise-mapping exercises, STI's teams would be busy, busy, busy. They would paper the walls with ideas and detailed flowcharts mapping material flows, duly notated with the hieroglyphics of storage and processing areas. Sometimes on these wall coverings material flows intersected information flows, the carefully delineated lines depicting key order activities such as color specification.

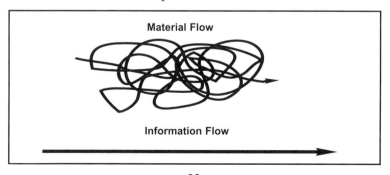

Deaux was never clear on whether these intersections were good or bad, but he feared that the messy collisions could be heard further down the Interstate. When the lines crossed frequently, the intersections produced a bizarre network of communication tangles. When the flows marched along happily in parallel, products appeared to move more quickly through the factory—no nasty inter-ruptions—but often the products were simply the wrong ones—bad configurations, unworkable flavors, all the messy variations that United's complex production machine, driven by an endlessly optimistic marketing plan, could muster. Deaux wasn't really sure how to deal with these kraft paper explorations of the extended enterprise, but he figured they kept people busy, and in his two-grand-per-hour world, busy meant happy.

For STI clients, even the evenings were tightly sched-uled. Debriefing and self-critiques, personality tests and group exercises left no time for drinking or other non-value-added group activities. Mental and physical exhaus-tion were a side-benefit of STI's well-regarded onsite cours-es, because Ed knew that when participants were faint and reeling from the sheer busyness of it all, no clients ques-tioned the true value of their offering. Deaux instructed all his lead instructors to keep moving, to never rest in the same spot for long, to stay unreachable, and above all, to start every team event at 6:30 AM. If approached, they were to press cell phones firmly to their ears and appear locked in critical conversations. And the formula seemed to be working. Typically one or two champions—it only took one—emerged from STI's executive training.

The next critical group of employees, the engineers, were a lingering scheduling challenge. Deaux had learned to sprinkle only two or three of these professionals into a team—more and the movement ground to a halt, fewer and the project jumped the rails.

The third and biggest group, Purchasing and

Production, had the least time to spare for training, but Deaux knew he could rely on his client, Dick Bufflelunk, to force sign-ups. That left Transportation and Logistics/Distribution, but who cared? Shippers were notoriously hard to handle, and they sub-optimized revenues anyway. The shop floor was his focus, and everyone else had just better fall in line.

Revenue projections firmed up and flooded STI's back-office receivables with black ink. Each one-week team experience, the showcase Spirit Project, cleared about $250,000, and Deux's training masters were booked through 2009.

Deaux had arrived. The receptionist ushered him into his clients' atrium waiting area while the consultant continued to punch cellphone numbers. Finally, Dick Bufflelunk emerged and wrapped a fat fist around Deaux' check-signing hand, "Great to see you again, old boy. We've reviewed the numbers, ID'd the problem areas, and I agree, we'll make the change. Let's start with Morgan."

Hail fellow well met

Morgan's invitations to Dick's staff meeting were as rare as May snow squalls. Nevertheless, the stars had aligned today for a promising meeting of the minds. Dick's assistant, Lynne, had summoned Morgan yesterday, two days into the new quarter. Morgan knew the Q4 results were not all tallied, but his figures showed that ship dollars had exceeded target by, give or take a couple cancellations and credit holds, a safe margin of $177,000.

At 8:56, still smiling from the post-quarter celebration down on the shipping docks—free Krispy Kremes for all—Steve Morgan took a seat at Dick's conference table. "I'm early," he thought, "as usual."

Lynne had thoughtfully set the side table with United Manufacturing napkins and glassware, a silver pitcher of ice water, bottled juices, and a tempting bowl of Swiss mints. Fresh notepads and pencils awaited. Morgan settled in. The silence was restful, his first quiet time since last week's end-of-quarter push.

9:05—A check-in with Admin Lynne—"They're on their way. There's been a call from the Chairman. Help yourself to fresh juice."

9:15—Another peek out at the office area, "Empty. Must be break time."

9:25—Voices in the hallway, footsteps passing close by. False alarm. Two young designers on their way to a teleconference, joking about last night's ball game.

9:27—Dick, United's CEO and protégé of United's founder, Captain Bob Crain, and his consultant, STI's, CEO Ed Deaux, glided in. Morgan straightened to attention. This was more than he expected—Ed Deaux was rumored to be the power behind the throne, but he had never met the man in person. "Hmm, shorter than I expected," he observed, reassured, sizing up the expert.

The meeting began with the usual pleasantries. "How's the family? Sorry we missed you at the holiday party. Who's your favorite to win the series?" Admin Lynne appeared and distributed a sheaf of numbers. "End-of-quarter ship notices," thought Steve. "More good news from the trenches."

"Steve," Dick Bufflelunk began, "I'm going to be frank with you. We've been reviewing your numbers. I know there are still a few shipments left to tally. But I've got to say, we are stunned."

Steve beamed and sat up still straighter, as if a small metal pincer attached to the back of his shirt collar were pulling him yet higher in his chair, making his continually extended neck three-quarters of an inch longer. "They know it, they see the results, they're impressed! I'm going to love it here! I might even take up tennis," he mused. An equestrian at heart, Morgan's signing bonus was rumored to have included an allowance to cover the cross-country transport of his dearest love, Beauty, a registered quarter horse, all the way from Albuquerque. But tennis, Morgan knew, was not beyond his physical talents—it was only a matter of time.

A comment from Deaux, seated at Dick's right hand, interrupted Morgan's reverie. "Yes, Steve. We've noticed a periodic deviation from the strategy we developed at the Orlando offsite. United's position as number two in the global motors market seems to be slipping. We think we have an execution problem. And that's why we called you here."

"What? The numbers…. Off the dock…. 100 percent?"

"That's right. An execution problem."

Morgan's basso inched up a few tones. "The numbers. The shipments. The results. All in, except for two last-minute cancellations. We made the ship numbers. We hit the target. It was a great year! My area shipped, in total for FY 05, $500M of product, ten percent above last year. Execution problem, my butt!"

Dick sighed deeply. This message was going to require higher volume.

"Yes, Steve, that's right. You made the ship numbers all right, but you blew the profit margin. United is still shipping more product than all of its competitors, but it's costing us 25 percent more than Electric Consolidated and 50 percent more than China."

Just to the left of his sternum, Morgan felt hot pliers pressing, squeezing. There, Dick had said it, the C word. The China price. Morgan knew that Asia had become a second source for some of his end customers, a riskier but easier solution to cost problems. Of course, he mumbled, you had to ship the parts across the Pacific or find and qualify local Asian suppliers. There was the added hassle of protecting United's new design portfolio while shipping detailed engineering drawings thousands of miles into the ozone—another counterfeiting opportunity. Pirates were everywhere. Who knew how that protocol went, but it made great business for the lawyers. Just try to enforce the Berne copyright convention ten thousand miles away! What's more, the shipments had to be processed and shipped over one potentially risky transportation mode after another—shipping containers, freight trains, bonded warehouses, even local short-run truckers. What's wrong with making and shipping it right here in the USA? Many of our customers are within earshot anyway. And what about quality? Everybody knows that for over 75 years United's motors—from the tiniest medical devices to the behemoths that powered giant utility plants—had the best quality. The United brand is accepted all over the world. We're the best! Exactly what is going on here?

Deaux flipped on the projector and aimed his laser pointer at the familiar United income statement. The red spot highlighted revenues, the product of a hundred years of diversification. United designs had created new markets, but as Marketing was proud to point out, there was still plenty more draw in traditional markets. Diversification spelled growth for United, and this year's results proved it.

Revenue from sales	$500M
Classic motor division (15%)	75M
Medical (12%)	60M
Automotive (28%)	140M
Heavy equipment (7%)	35M
Consumer goods (7%)	35M
Marine (5%)	25M
Aerospace (8%)	40M
Aftermarket (5%)	25M
Lawn and garden (3%)	15M
Electronics (5%)	25M
Utilities (5%)	25M

"Sure, we've all seen these a thousand times," Morgan protested. "What's the point? Move on."

"I'll do just that, Steve." Dick Bufflelunk moved the cursor, and up popped the numbers that most held Steve's interest—cost of goods sold, specifically purchased materials and in-house manufacturing.

Cost of goods sold:
Cost of purchased goods and services
(55 % of sales) $275M
Manufacturing in-house (33 %) $165M

"Ah yes," thought Steve, we arrive at what counts, making shipments, the story of manufacturing. "Looking good."

The red dot moved down through other cost contributors—engineering, marketing and administrative functions. Finally, the laser locked in on the bottom line, zero.

Engineering and R & D (6%) $30M
SG&A (Selling, general and
Administrative) (6%) $30M

Profit   0

"Zero profit? What? But . . . That can't be," Steve sputtered. "We made the quarter. We shipped more orders, more line items off the dock last week than United has in its 100-year history! My guys set the dollars shipped record! What is this?"

Deaux nodded and nudged his client. Morgan knew it was time to sit down and listen.

The consultant took over. "You see, Steve, over the past two years United has been experiencing margin creep that is squeezing revenues in some product areas. The accountants have reviewed your expenses, and they find direct and

indirect costs going up. In fact, United's average production and material costs are up anywhere from five to 25
percent. It's a trend that can't continue, because it's costing
us customers. You've got to find a way to bring down costs
15 percent this year and 20 percent next. We've got to generate some profit."

The CEO's eyes bored into Morgan's face. "Steve, I
want you front and center on this. It's time to call in the
accumulated goodwill that United has built up with its
workforce and the suppliers. You've got nine months—
three quarters—to do it. Otherwise, the stockholders and
the family will revolt. They'll demand far harsher measures. And we know we all don't want that. And the union
won't stand for it.

"Steve, as the primary contributor to product costs, it's
up to you. Deaux and I will give you all the help we can.
We've got you and all your people scheduled in for Spirit
Master Kaizen classes starting next week. We'll be running
our first pilot this coming quarter. After we've trained
every in-house employee, we'll take on the supply base.
I'm excited! It's the kind of total, absolute culture change
that United's next generation needs."

"Deaux assures me that when you've all completed his
training, even the lowest material handler will be energized
and a true Spirit Master. You'll be cutting waste everywhere, from setups to production runs. Even the electricity
bills will plummet. I've just returned from STI's premier
Spirit Master conference, and I can't wait to get started. On
just our one pilot area we reduced inventories by 30 percent.
We cut cycle time 20 percent. Quality rejects dropped by
half. And that's just the beginning. The guys over at
MetalWorksCo are on their twelfth kaizen project, and their
results are phenomenal. I'm excited. Let's talk again after
you've finished your Third Degree Spirit Master training.

"Good luck to you, Steve, And thanks for coming down
here today."

Chapter 3
Lean, leaner, leanest

"More weight."
Last words of Giles Corey, while being
crushed to death as a result of his wrongful
conviction at the Salem Witch trials

By the time Morgan's Suburban pulled into the United lot, the word was out. "Something wrong with the numbers—costs, margins eroding. It's the Japanese. The Koreans. The maquiladoras. The Chinese. They're talking layoffs. Pay cuts. Offshoring."

Fear infected the plant like a bad cold that started with chills, some sneezes, and progressed to full-blown bronchial pneumonia. Breathing was hard. The pressure on everyone's chest seemed immovable. Morgan felt the chill as well, and a quick walk through the warehouse confirmed it. "I can always count on Carl Morilla," the warehouse supervisor, he thought, for the real skinny. Carl had worked his way up from material handler to warehouse supervisor. He knew everyone, heard everything. But Carl had been carted off to the local ER this noon—chest pains. Steve walked a lonely path back to his office.

When he called for messages, his assistant averted her eyes. There were none, just a reminder from STI's client scheduler that Morgan's executive Master Spirit classes were on for next Monday at 7 AM.

The week passed quickly enough, and by Wednesday, Morgan began to anticipate Monday's first United Executive Master class. Having survived several high-tech wars, Morgan believed in back-up plans. Just in case, he wanted to pull in some supplier cost reductions right away. He would send his crack buyer/planners out to renegotiate or otherwise squeeze key supplier contracts. If Dick wanted 15 percent, 15 percent was what he would get.

"Annie, get Brendanne and Candyman in here for purchase order contract review. And run me a full cost printout of the biggest-dollar suppliers."

Brendanne Soufflet worked two doors away from Steve Morgan in a stripped-down corner cubicle furnished with the usual purchasing tools—laptop, printer, two cell phones, a pager, one Blackberry, and a coffee mug filled with Day-Glo highlighters. Morgan knew when Brendanne rounded the corner to his office. Her musky, tropical cologne infused the area with the heavy scent of dark Asian blossoms and woods. Hmmm. Still trim after two-and-a-half years in Operations, Brendanne excited Morgan's curiosity. She carried a certain exotic reputation among her peers that Steve would have explored had it not been for her mysterious steady beau.

Brendanne's friends were few, but her male admirers were many. Women were a different matter, however. Women noticed the little quirks that made Brendanne's total package just one millimeter off—the way she wore the wrong color red with a maroon suit, the fact that her left ring finger—"the wrong finger" they said— sported a one-carat solitaire she described as a "non-engagement friendship ring," the way she climbed stairs sideways in her two-inch heels—"ridiculous," they said, "the broad can't walk straight!"—as if she were afraid of missing a tread and bumping indecorously down to the bottom, a feat she had actually accomplished one day in 1999 during an inspection tour.

Her voice was remarkable for its absence. Few at the plant recalled hearing her speak, though one security guard claimed that her "Open this door right now" had a certain breathy quality appropriate to one with her airy surname, Soufflet, which he'd been told was French for "to breathe . . . to moan." He liked that. Brendanne's over-whelming communications mode preference was digital—Blackberry or laptop. Safer and cleaner, she thought, with predictable results that left no wiggle room for imprecise responses. She had little use for the human voice—or the human face, for that matter.

"Take a seat, my dear. You're looking fit and chipper this morning."

"Umhh," she replied, her mouth working to squeeze down one last bagel bite.

"Blondie—uh, Brendanne—as you know, we've all done a super job out here getting suppliers on board and ramping up production. For the sixth quarter in a row we beat the ship target. But I've got to tell you, this week I've had some ugly surprises."

"Mmmf," she added, nodding twice. "Go on, get to it, Morgan," she thought.

"Ah, yes, that's it," Morgan added, realizing he'd hit on a magic formula to deliver tough messages, the sandwich technique. Give them the good news first—"Hey guys, great job, you made the quarter!" and then hit 'em with the kicker, "But you blew the profits. Corporate is not pleased, and we've got to turn it around."

Brendanne nodded and reached for her vibrating cell phone. The display urgently pulsed area code 212—Manhattan. She itched to take the call.

Undeterred, Morgan continued. "Yes, we made the quarter and set a new United ship record. But our costs are too high and margins are slipping. We've got to cut costs."

Brendanne's eyes widened. How did Ol' Morgan figure it out? She had seen this moment coming 18 months back when steel suppliers hiked prices, and oil price increases cascaded down through the plastics markets, but she thought it would be at least another four months before Morgan got wind of it. No matter. Everything, she had learned from her old mentor, was negotiable, up to the moment the assembly line started to move.

"United suppliers love us," Morgan said. "They know how we play the game. And we've stood by them for years. But tough times call for tougher measures. We've got to cut our costs. If they can't do it, another supplier will."

Brendanne gulped. Ol' Morgan meant business!

"That's why we have 30,000 of them! Our suppliers love us, and we're going to make the numbers. Any questions?" Morgan's raised eyebrows elicited silence, which he took as complete agreement.

"Well, that's decided. Now then," Morgan resumed, moving rapidly toward a cheery sendoff. "I want you and Candyman to hightail it out to these suppliers"—he handed Brendanne a three-inch-thick printout of United's purchasing requirements. Morgan had color-coded his targets—356 key suppliers were highlighted in hot pink. The second group of 2,015 suppliers, Steve called them B candidates, were marked in yellow, signifying caution; these were longtime suppliers whom United had always counted on to be there. And the remaining group Steve admittedly knew nothing about, but where they seemed to represent late orders or unknown SKUs, he had high-lighted them in blue—"blue for exploration," he thought.

Brendanne's gaze moved to the door. Her cell continued to blink and buzz. "Damn, those headhunters sure are persistent. We'll soon see who's gonna win this race." For the past month Brendanne and her buddy down in engineering, Billy Mac, had been in a race to see who could exit United first.

Billy had almost won the race prematurely last year when he found himself working for the wrong manager. Young Billy had a sweet innocence and compassion about him that United had all but squeezed out. He still needed, he was told on that last day in the warehouse, to learn stronger supervisory methods—in other words, when to get tough. Billy would never learn, and Brendanne loved, well, liked him for it.

Billy's father, Mac Senior, had started a small placement firm specializing in purchasing, production and materials people, and she strongly suspected that Senior's succession plan was about to be put into action. Which would take Billy out of United forever. It was an unfair advantage, but she had other things pulling for her.

Brendanne hit the speed dial number of Heinrich Strong, Inc., one of five headhunters who were on her "Do not block" list. Time to check in. This was one race she had no intention of losing

Ed Candyman, back from his Midwest expediting trip, waited in Morgan's conference room, next up. Last week's end-of-month rush had added ten points to his blood pressure. His cheeks were stretched tight, bright cherry red, and his ankles felt fat. Candyman liked to think he was in excellent physical condition, but younger staffers knew that that time had passed several career moves back. Now here was a moment to take a breather, to let the ankles settle out.

Morgan reappeared. "Ed, so good to see you. How about coffee? Or would you like a Coke?" Ed took his third black coffee of the day and settled in, readying his brightest smile for the end-of-quarter applause. He knew Steve liked to backslap his guys, so he remained seated to eliminate that option—he didn't want to lose air pressure. Still, it was clear something was on Morgan's mind.

"Ed, we've got ourselves a situation here. Corporate says we've got to cut costs, and I couldn't agree more. Trouble is, it's a little late in the game. We don't have much time. I decided to put my best guy on the job. Ed, starting this Monday, you're on temporary roving assignment. I want you out there with the suppliers taking down their contract prices. Call them new contracts, call them rebates, call them invoice errors, but we've got to bring purchased material costs down at least 15 percent. RB says we have nine months before the stockholders revolt. I'm counting on you. I've instructed Annie to get you travel money—will eight thousand be enough to get you started? Give me a call when you get to Kuala Lumpur. Don't worry about your commodities—I've handed them over to Wheeney. You and Blondie—er, Brendanne—are excused from Master Kaizen training. We'll get you into class when you get back. Good luck!"

The 15 percent (or more) solution

Next up, administrivia—overtime and business travel. Steve knew that a war on costs could be partially fought with psychology, so he decided to keep everyone's focus on cost reductions. Freezing overtime and business travel—no trips without his sign-off—would emphasize the seriousness of United's challenge. A cost containment directive also meant, of course, that raises and bonuses would be sparingly doled out.

Time for his three o'clock status meeting. Staffers arrived and silently took their places.

"Folks, listen up. We've got a situation here. Corporate's in trouble. We've posted record ship numbers, but costs are biting into profits and we've had some margin slippage. We've got to cut costs at least 15 percent this year."

("No sense giving them the full details just yet. Let's just see what they can do to take costs down a few percentage points")

Heads nodded. This message was not without precedent—it was just a question of percentages, and Morgan's staff was willing to wait. Every one of them had his own back-up plan, parts buried in the Field Service bins, a buddy out at a couple suppliers, an order floating in permanent limbo, ready to be pulled in to make target. Even Wade Jackman down in shipping had a spare trucking container just in case. They knew that Morgan knew—it was part of the game, and it was gonna stay that way! When the next end-of-quarter rush came, things would happen.

Morgan continued. "Next week we're launching our Spirit Master Kaizen training. I'll be in the first class, and each of you will have a chance to take the training and do a pilot. We want to be first in on this incredible approach to culture change. It's going to take 20, 25, maybe 30 percent or more out of our production costs. Pick up your packets and schedules from Annie. No waivers. Dismissed."

That task completed, Morgan pulled out his Master Kaizen kit. The plastic book bag held two energy bars, one chocolate kiss, two pairs of nylons, one Army issue compass, matches, 20 condoms, a notepad, drawing/engineering paper, a stopwatch, and number-two drawing pencils.

"Gheesh, a fella could have a good weekend in Vegas with this stuff!" he thought.

Time to prep for his first class.

It was a strange beginning. Monday morning, Morgan found himself in a small war room right alongside the assembly line, where Deaux and his lead instructor, Tom Bender, were setting up a projector and flip charts.

Deaux explained that each team member would learn the basic kaizen methods used by the Toyota Production and the Honda BP pull systems. They would learn how to observe, to take data, to plot results, to highlight bottlenecks and waste and to brainstorm solutions that met the basic rules of kaizen. They would build a heijunka box out of cardboard and Kraft paper and decorate it with brightly colored order numbers. Then they would design a new production area.

Next, Bender took the class through slides depicting 5S, poke-yoke, pull systems, kanban, standard work, and cell vs. assembly-line design. It was a lot to cover. After break, the group studied the value stream map of a traditional furniture maker. A short course in how to use the stopwatch, and the group was almost ready to hit the floor. The only missing piece was the project, a manufacturing problem area that Deaux and Bender had selected; the team would learn exactly what this was tomorrow morning.

Deaux warned the class that by Wednesday they must be well into a workable solution—a pilot —that would reduce inventories and cut throughput times. Thursday noon was the project deadline; on Friday, the team would present. Critiques from the experts, followed by a grand end-of-project celebration, distinguished this approach from traditional industrial engineering. The event would wrap up by Friday at noon.

"You'll need notepads, pencils and your stopwatches. We're going on a walk," Deaux concluded. Morgan's fellow team members clustered around their instructor as they walked through the plant, working backwards from the shipping dock to upstream operations—past cages, tool cribs, feeder lines, small-parts storage areas. They passed pallets piled with tagged parts, rejects, some incomplete assemblies awaiting disposition. In one corner stacks of cardboard and metal strapping— inbound material packaging debris—stood 15 feet high. Forklifts sped by. Some drivers nodded at the unusual assemblage of visitors, each clutching a stopwatch and notepad.

Line of sight

Their first stop was the shipping dock. Jackman had been warned to expect visitors. That was not unusual—Jack recognized them, except for their short, dark-suited leader. Deaux held the group's attention, using animated hand motions and pointing toward a side conveyor where hot shipments received individual attention. The class scribbled in their notebooks and moved over into the main aisle.

The classic motor assembly line had slowed. Two operators stood nearby. One of them, Joe Callahan, was holding a complete unit. He picked up another from the line, looked it over, and put both on a cart. The top shelf was filled with red-tagged items; these units weren't going anywhere. Joe turned back to the line and picked up where he left off. The conveyor continued to move. Down at the last operation, Jackman's packers were readying shipping boxes and liners, but there was a holdup. Instruction manuals were stacked next to the shipping boxes. As soon as a motor reached the end of its conveyor ride, an operator checked its housing against the customer order, applied a stamp to the housing, selected a manual in the right language for the customer and moved the whole kit down the line. The packers had completed two boxes, and they were waiting for the next batch of motors matched with orders and manuals. But nothing was happening. Time for Dottie L., Jack's shipping supervisor, to hustle up some more of the right manuals.

The team observed all these activities. They continued to take notes, hoping they were capturing the key levers that would make this line sing.

Back in the war room, it was time for the team to develop a plan. Morgan took the floor. "The problem is the line fill rate," he said. "The forecast for these motors was 240 per day. But we've only been able to produce 200 on a good day. I counted at least 30 in various stages of completion And there was that cart filled with rejects—I don't know what those units were doing or who owns them. One of the tags on the bottom shelf was dated last February! We've got a capacity problem"

"Yeah, Steve," seconded Amy, the junior cost accountant. "It looked like things were sort of bottled up at the end of the line. Why weren't there enough manuals?"

John Tiekman, the engineering draftsman, thought he saw a different problem further upstream. "One of the motors seemed to have the wrong housing. I heard one operator telling the expeditor to call the foreman for a replacement. I think we have a stockroom problem."

"No," responded Morgan, "it's an operator problem. The materials are there, they just have to use the right ones."

Tom Bender listened quietly while the team attacked the problem from differing vantage points. He would not give them the solution, but he knew which questions would cause them to take the right data.

"All right, folks. Those are good observations. But I think you need to go further. Remember the value stream map we showed before lunch? If you can't express what's happening to a production process with your stopwatches and note pads, you're not really seeing. Let the data lead you." With that, Tom left the war room.

"What kind of answer was that?" everyone asked. The team members shifted uncomfortably. The temperature rose a few degrees, and Morgan felt his string tie tighten. There wasn't much time to observe, plan a solution and execute, but that was exactly what Bender seemed to be telling them to do. Morgan repeated "We've got to fix the capacity problem right now!"

Amy piped up. She was green, having never spent an hour on the production floor, but she knew a good number when she saw one. And she believed that fifteen minutes alone out there would get them more numbers than they could count. "I'm taking myself out to the line" she said. "I'm volunteering for observer duty."

Not to be outdone by the kid, Morgan offered to track down kit quantities and shortages. He wanted to see what the true shortages were for this operation, and where the material flows broke down.

John and Terry were eager to map the process and lay out a new flow. They wanted to break down the 200-foot, conveyor-driven assembly line and set up one of those new production cells Tom Bender had described. But where to begin? The process would be disruptive, even to an area that had just completed a massive shipping quarter. Something about the difference between batch flows and single-unit production stuck. If one cell built one complete unit, start to finish, the quality and shortage problems would be pretty visible and immediate. No work, no flow, no product. John was not sure the volumes would be higher than a well-run assembly line, but those volumes weren't smooth flows, either. What's to lose by playing with the idea a bit more?

Tom Bender reappeared just in time. "Uh, guys?" he interjected. "Remember that takt time calculation we studied? Well, this might be just the right time to drag out your calculators and take a look at what the production rate is supposed to be. Forget the forecast for now. What do the customers want?"

Aha, another useful clue from the sensei. The team members stopped for a moment and the room began to buzz.

"Hey, that's a clue! Bender's telling us we can build a cell, and it doesn't have to go faster than the line. In fact, I bet when we calculate takt time, it's nothing close to what the old line was set up to run."

"Still, I don't get the thing about one cell that does every operation. And the assemblers have to stand up all the time. And where are the material handlers in this equation?"

"Level loading, level loading," Amy said. "The forecast runs up and down like the Salisbury roller coaster, but we've got to level-load the plant? I don't get it. Can we tell our customers to level-load their orders?"

Questions filled the air as team members, overwhelmed with the possibilities, headed toward the vending machines. Potato chips and chocolate would clarify this picture.

STI had supplied the team with more than stopwatches and note pads. Over in the corner were a complete tool box, scrap lumber and nail guns. Evidently, Morgan observed, they expect us to build something.

"John," Morgan called. "Take a look at this stuff. We've got everything we need to build a pilot cell!"

Now this was more like it. Team members John and Terry unpacked the tool kit and started a shopping list. They would have to hit Home Depot for the remaining items—plywood, a rubber mat, some sheet metal and shears, and a couple spray cans. John had a vision, which he quickly sketched out. Everyone gathered around his drawing as the plan began to take shape.

"Look, the assembly line is broke. They want us to try a pull system and do production in a cell. The only way to do that is to set up some tables and simulate assembly from parts stocked on the line, and then to pack and seal the boxes right here!" John marked the spot where boxes would be sealed for shipping.

"That's right, John. What they want is a complete cell, no batched flows or partial assemblies or motor components. One part, one assembly, one motor, one label, one line item. Next part, housing, screws, motor, pack." Steve beat out the rhythm of a pilot cell. "It sure doesn't sound like Henry Ford's River rouge assembly line, but what the heck, we might learn something here, and it beats another day at the desk!"

Amy hustled back to the War Room after her lonely line observation time. "Guys, you won't believe what I saw. That line keeps running because of the expeditors. One minute it's running parts about every 30 seconds, and the next it's doing nothing. This is crazy!" she said. "Does anybody know what the real takt time is?"

Three more team members rushed out to the line for baseline studies. They wanted to see for themselves what was causing the delays. They weren't disappointed.

Tuesday at five, the group reconvened to lay out Wednesday's plan. Tiekman shared his concept of a production cell. Amy added her takt time calculations. Morgan offered his carpentry assistance, while the others started gathering materials.

Wednesday morning, construction began hurriedly. A quick sketch of the cell included plastic bins to deliver just the right number of motor components. One by one, each team member disassembled a complete motor, then reassembled it to discover the work breakdown.

It was time for STI's Tom Bender to have a look. "Well, you're on the right track," he said, "If you can break down the process and simulate the assembly motions, and then figure out how to deliver the right quantity of parts, you'll have it." Though the team knew there would be more to designing and simulating a real cell, at least they knew they were headed in the right direction.

Thursday's cell simulation moved quickly. Amy, "The Kid," was volunteered as their first assembler. The team struggled with an assembly fixture design that would hold the motor so that it was easier for the assembler to attach screws. But they wanted to learn how to control parts inventories without expeditors, and they needed to design a supermarket parts system that positioned everything the assembler needed at just the right height.

The plan was that parts would be certified for immediate line-side delivery from suppliers—not batched through long receiving and inspection operations. The whole rhythm of parts movement and assembly work was designed to follow takt times, a steady and comfortable pace. The team planned for fewer quality problem interruptions caused by bad parts. That meant that the suppliers had to be on board with United's new quality requirements. When one defective component appeared, the operator would stop, flag the problem, and resume assembly with a replacement. Disposition was immediate. The part was set aside for evaluation by the supplier. It was a perfect plan.

Thursday afternoon, the team was eager to try out their

mock cell, time it and prepare final presentations. They'd learned how to measure an assembly operation's efficiency: parts per hour per person before and parts per hour per person after. Their observation and data collection skills had been tuned up.

Team members prepared for the trial, stopwatches at the ready. Amy was positioned inside the cell. "Go!" shouted Morgan, and the kid began to assemble a finished classic motor. Her right hand reached for a housing and coil. Four other components were arranged in assembly sequence in plastic tubs. After Amy had inserted the parts, she positioned the bottom housing in its fixture, popped on the top cover, and started to close it up. Three screws inserted beautifully. The fourth and fifth did not fit. All production stopped. Minutes ticked by as Steve and John searched for the right size fasteners.

Amy searched for other assemblies to work on while the correct screws were hunted down. But the team had not set up batches of unfinished assemblies and there were no other products on her build list. Even the shipping box and manual were ready. There was little for her to do but wait. The seconds ticked into minutes. She knew the motor could not ship incomplete, and it was frustrating. Finally, Dottie appeared with two bags of missing screws, and the race resumed.

The second motor assembly went smoother for Amy. All parts were within reach, she was getting the hang of the nifty fixture, and team members excitedly cheered her on. Two more assemblies, and it was time for the others to take a turn in the hot seat, then back to the war room for a working lunch.

Tomorrow's presentation would be a first opportunity for the team members to deliver big solutions to United's manufacturing challenges. Everyone was eager to share the excitement, the potential that lay in this approach. "But," warned Morgan, "we've got to speak with numbers. It's the only way to sell continued kaizen projects. Let's pull together a spreadsheet of pilot savings."

"You're right," piped up Amy, fresh from two powerful new production experiences, her first. "We know we reduced inventory, our cell takes less space, we need fewer people, and I have a feeling we won't want expeditors. By my rough calculations, we've got about a 25 percent inventory reduction, 20 percent savings in space, and overall head count reduction of 30 percent. Plus we can probably drop the third shift!"

"Wow," said John. "Think of what United could do with the savings! We could fund a whole new product line. Maybe even go after some business in South America."

"So it's agreed. We'll finish the spreadsheet, put John's cell design on the flip chart, do a dry run, and break for dinner."

Chapter 4
On the road again . . .

> Squeeze me, baby, like a crash test dummy.
> Beat me, baby, eight to the bar.

"Oooh."
"Aaah."
"Oooh."
"Aaah."
"Umm. Oh, yes, just like that. Oh no, no-o-o-o. Oh yes, do it right there, aah, more Blondie, more."
"Mmmf—aeeee!"

Blondie rolled over, reached for a cigarette and hit the room service button for Suite 317 of Singapore's five-star best. Such rigorous exercise not only released those precious happy endorphins, she was famished! She lit a Gaulois and settled back on the pillows to breathe.

"Hand me that notepad, would you, dearest?" Dick Bufflelunk ordered.

"Still thinks he's back in the office." she noted silently, as she tapped cigarette ashes onto the room service tray. Bits of tandoori, prime rib, Parker House rolls, matchbooks from every five-star hotel in East Asia, used condom wrappers and an extra slice of mocha torte littered the night stand. This is a girl with big appetites— men, boys, prime ribs, electric motors.

"How does this sound for an opener, Blondie?" Dick asked, eager for encouragement and applause.

"When I was asked to give the keynote for this august trade group, I searched for a way to convey the excitement we at United are experiencing growing new global markets. Just yesterday, my Operations VP phoned with the results. We are completely booked through next year, and the economy is not yet back to full steam.

"But I want to share with you some serious concerns I have about our ability to satisfy new markets. It's all about our suppliers. We're counting on you to deliver higher quality at lower prices than ever before. It's the only way we can together offer the most competitive prices.

"That's why I have asked my top procurement pros to get on the road and visit each and every one of you. Because we value our supplier relationships and we are trusting you to work together with us to deliver the kind of competitive products that will continue to capture customer orders."

The Industrial Suppliers Association annual dinner meeting would kick off that night with Dick Bufflelunk's keynote speech. Although Brendanne loved these affairs— long tables stacked with hors d'oeuvres, rich whipped-cream cake, tortes, glazed fruits, spicy bites of salami, hot roasted nuts and free drinks—she would make just a brief solo appearance, then retire to prep tomorrow's supplier meetings, the first of 23 on this Far East encampment. And she needed to get back to catch up with the latest head-hunter messages—the 12-hour time difference was inconvenient, but it also gave her more room to maneuver among suitors.

Still, that new cell phone ring could be annoying. Steve's number appeared again on the display—he'd dogged her unsuccessfully through LAX, Tokyo, and now here he was trying to reach her in Singapore. Doesn't the man ever sleep?

Blondie, aka Brendanne, sighed and wrapped a thick hotel robe around her toned body. Thank God for personal trainers, the only way a girl would survive three years at United. "Hi Steve," she typed into her Palm. "LAX fine. Tokyo great. Taiwan next. More next week. Bye.

Brendanne." "That should hold him," she thought as she punched the Send button.

Back at United, Morgan's top reports were completing STI's introductory Spirit Master Kaizen class. Two more teams had completed demo projects; there were only another two dozen or so groups remaining on the training schedule. Morgan was encouraged by results. Every new kaizen celebration engaged a few more key people. With luck, the initiative would reach Engineering before winter snows covered the parking lot. Culture change was a new challenge for United—Steve could feel the tiny earth tremors already.

Brendanne stepped up to the curb. The concierge had carefully arranged drivers for her first round of supplier consults. The doorman ushered her to a waiting black sedan. There was just time enough to check e-mails from the headhunters, another call from Morgan and the stock quotes for today's opening. She was on her way.

TOP Supply had been United's primary vendor for over eight years, supplying tiny motor components and regulators. TOP was a dependable supplier whose capacity grew with United's bigger customer base. Although TOP's prices were not always the lowest, their cooperative approach to deliveries was a strong point. But things were changing.

Brendanne began. "United markets have opened up. There is so much more volatility. United needs more flexibility from their suppliers and lower prices—15 percent lower, in fact. We're counting on you," she said, as she picked up her pen and noted contract price changes. A rebate from TOP would take three percent off this year's annual bill, or about $150,000. "Not good enough. Next year will have to be a lot better."

Her second stop took more time, but proved more fruitful. Island Electronics was a new supplier to United. A team of Island production managers greeted her in the lobby, along with the new president, Winston Chu. Brendanne was ushered into the executive conference room, where refreshments and a display of new products awaited.

"What can Island do for you?" began Chu, who already knew of United's 15 percent cost reduction quest.

Brendanne smiled and punched up a slide showing United's marketing forecast. "We're here to share upcoming business projections," she answered, pointing to sales projections, a straight line that climbed with the thrust of a Saturn rocket, up and off the charts. "We believe we're going to crack the South American market. We've got about a nine-month window to do it in, and incidentally, as you can see, we're talking a 50 percent increase in shipments. " She paused and smiled. "Steve Morgan and I really hope Island can support this enormous increase. We'd like to see a corresponding decrease in Island prices, effective this fiscal year. We'd like to be able to shift more component orders to Island. That will require a very competitive pricing strategy." Smooth, she thought, it's a price cut linked with higher volumes squeeze. If they don't buy it, I walk. Brendanne hit the speed dial for her limo driver as she pulled her attaché case closer.

Chu did not hesitate. "Yes, Ms. Soufflet, you may recall that our original partnership strategy called for us to ramp up shipments to United. We think we are right on target to do that. We have completed two high-volume production areas, and we are ready to commit to your new order at what we think is a very competitive price. I will let our contracts guy go over the details, the cancellation penalty—15 percent—cost escalation clauses, restocking fees. Island has a great solution for your growing market needs, and we're happy that United has chosen Island to grow with."

"Hmm," Brendanne thought. "A 15 percent penalty clause. Raw material cost escalations passed through to United? Restocking charges? Well, no matter, I'll be long gone by then!"

"Fine," she said. "Send us the paperwork, and we'll be in touch. Great doing business with you!"

Messages from the US piled up at the concierge's desk. Brendanne's private cell phone buzzed, and her laptop's e-mail count stood at 127. She was due at the airport in two hours for her flight to Taiwan. There was just enough time to grab lunch and skip the noon checkout. Her driver called. He was waiting in the lobby.

Morgan would be pleased to hear trip results.

"Productive trip," she punched. "Savings, increased volume shift to Island, 15 percent costs down, next stop Taiwan." That should keep him happy.

Happy would not describe Morgan's dead eyes and shell-shocked visage. Although the master classes were going well—there was great buzz in the plant about takt time and cells, level loading and the quest for lean—Steve felt a tightening in his chest every time he reviewed shipping figures. The booking rate and kit release rates were close, but shortages were climbing twice as fast as the backlog. Some orders were two weeks old, yet crates of component boxes overflowed receiving. The whole plant felt fat and logy, like Thanksgiving after the big meal. He wanted to loosen his tie and take off his belt. .

Dick Bufflelunk's 15 percent cost reduction target loomed. Morgan saw movement in the pilot cells, especially in the area of inventory reduction. The teams had decreased the cardboard piles, and every pilot cell was designed with lineside racks, supermarkets stocked with small components. The plant certainly looked cleaner. One more month and the pilot teams would report in on key end-of-quarter metrics—inventories, productivity and cycle time. It was hard to wait.

Meanwhile, Morgan's back-up purchasing strategy was proceeding nicely. Candyman and Brendanne had made a dozen supplier visits, though their trip reports were somewhat sketchy. "Yes, there are many ways to achieve supplier cost reductions—rebates, repricing, new business quotes—but the bottom line for United was still 15 percent cost down this year. Perhaps," he speculated, "their combined price savings would hit seven to ten percent. Hard to tell."

Carl Morilla, looking ripe for another bout of chest pains, interrupted Morgan's shipping reveries. "Steve, yesterday I pulled this unit off the line. Incoming QC passed it, but the vendor ain't certified. I don't know what happened, but it looks like every United Manufacturing Classic made since last month has a component problem. Intermittent failures and sudden death. Al Kantargis in Field Service is getting the calls."

"What?"

"That's right. Failures in the field and problems on the line. Don't know how, but somebody screwed the pooch."

Cold steel pliers slipped under Steve's shirt and squeezed off another slice of his guts. Steve felt like Prometheus, the Greek Titan whose liver was pecked away nightly by vultures, each painful regeneration foretelling yet another nocturnal visit from the birds of prey who tormented him. "How much longer would this go on?" he thought as he reached for the Mylanta.

Chapter 5
Little Heroes

> This ain't no party
> This ain't no disco
> This ain't no foolin' around.
> —The Talking Heads

All around the plant, United Manufacturing workers and managers settled into numb, shocked routine—ship product, schedule a little overtime, work the weekend, pull in the next week's work, work the shortages, ship product. Minor heroes stepped up to multiple challenges. Jackman pulled in parts from other divisions, Field Service's Kantargis located truckloads of forgotten parts to replace blemished ones. Morilla abandoned his stockroom for assembly duties. Overnight, a fire at a key supplier, Northwest Plastics, united everyone when a simple cost reduction edict couldn't. Northwest burned down to the cellar, losing all in-process production, the previous week's completed finished goods, and just about everything else, including two trailers parked at the loading dock.

Morning meetings at United took on a desperate, sharper focus as Jackman and his team tallied up each day's possible shipments. As soon as that task was done, planners searched the data base for other possible complete configurations. No one knew if the end result would satisfy customers, but everyone lived with the first rule of manufacturing—make something happen! Build it! Pack it! Ship it!

And the kaizen master training continued. "A blessed distraction," thought Morgan as he made his way to a team meeting where the pilot cell neared completion. Team members welcomed the respite. In this perfect world, a pull system set priorities for production and material flows. Here, no five-alarm fires, no broken-down trucks, no demanding customers, no blizzards or bankruptcies intruded. Team members could calculate takt time and design a production cell to meet just exactly that level-loaded pace. Excess inventories melted away. Even the operators, once they realized their jobs would be upgraded to include less repetition and more variety, were eager to try out the pilot. Here, in this one very thin slice of a global supply chain that stretched six tiers deep and thousands of miles wide, there were no disruptions from Mother Nature or arson. Everything ran according to The Plan. It was, Morgan thought grimly, about as close to Utopia as he would ever get.

The hourly countdown proceeded. At week's end, Morgan tallied up shipments against targets. But cost figures were slower to develop. When shipping paperwork cleared the system, Cost Accounting calculated actual incurred costs, order by order and product group by product group. The process took several days to run, but the final numbers carried great weight with all United workers.

Though Dick's phone calls were less frequent, he also tracked ship dollars. Steve knew that this quarter's total was running about 20 percent below the run rate at this time last year. He also saw from Blondie's growing stack of room service tabs that the push to negotiate new purchased parts deals continued. With over 30,000 suppliers worldwide, it was Morgan's job to pick the handful of critical suppliers whose invoice costs could make a significant contribution to profits.

Still, it was not enough. By the time Dick redeployed Morgan, another, bigger threat appeared, one that even the best expeditors could not overcome: China—three billion souls hungry to join the pseudo-capitalist ranks of the happily squeezed middle class.

The memo was simple enough.

UNITED MANUFACTURING

Dear United colleagues,

    I know you all share with me your appreciation for the time and service of Steve Morgan. Steve will be joining a crack team of engineers in our Amazon South American plant, where he is expected to bring considerable energies to growing this market segment.

    In the interim, I have appointed Sieg Wolfe director of operations, reporting directly to my office. Sieg's responsibilities will include local purchasing, manufacturing and logistics. Sieg will be joining all of you in Master Spirit Kaizen training. I cannot emphasize enough how important it is for all of us to continue this culture change. We know that by reducing inventories at all levels, seeking out waste and redeploying excess workers, we will achieve the company's 15 percent cost reduction target.

                   Best of luck to you all!

                 Robert Crain
                 Chairman of the Board,
                 United Manufacturing

The cafeteria hummed with the news. Morgan was out, their own Wolfe in. Top management focus was riveted on United's performance results. Among the lunch tables the rumor mill and stomachs churned— "Freeze on overtime. We've got quality problems. We need to stop and fix the assembly line. Where are we going to get parts?" The anxious buzz circulated rumor and fact equally quickly. Today's news bulletin cited a bit of good news from Northwest Plastics. Gross and Marino's heroic retrieval of damaged molds had proven out. Johnson, Northwest's owner, persuaded a nearby facility to rebuild the molds, and they were now in transit to a new supplier. The move was expensive and time-consuming—but there were no other options, and line-down situations cost the company thousands of dollars per hour. If United were going to keep production running Stateside, tooling and materials had to remain here.

Sean Bittbeiter slid a tray of French fries and chili over to the end of the table. Sean had noticed more animated conversations in the parking lot, and he knew from watching his ERP screens that the production landscape was shifting. Invoice prices for his electronic components had dropped a few percentage points. Still, the customer order backlog climbed, along with several weeks' worth of finished goods on hand. Production struggled to ship what was buildable. It was a strange alignment of opposing forces, one that Sean felt would lead to unanticipated results.

Bittbeiter's new blog entries netted undercurrents of fear and anxiety at United. Every night after the junior buyer finished checking world commodity index prices against his commodity list, he scanned the blog. The circle of respondents was widening as more on-line mavens arrived to talk up the latest developments. "The Scribes' revenge," he called it. Just as Gutenberg's printing press had destroyed the monks' hand-publishing monopoly 500 years ago, his Internet blogs would blast away at corporate information brokering and denial. The blog was not just another web-based information source, it was a giant myth builder and destroyer.

Technology rules! Bittbeiter found the master kaizen classes boring and oversimplified. "This world," he knew, "is filled with complexity and chaos, and the only way to survive it is to have more information than your competitors. And my Blogosphere will prove it."

Dick closed the door, told Lynne to hold all calls, and

took a seat opposite his new operations head, Siegfried Wolfe.

"Wolfie, I don't need to tell you how critical manufacturing and purchasing operations are for United. Last quarter's results were ugly. Our ship numbers were high, but costs were even higher. We can't continue this way. I'm looking to you to pull us out of the ditch. "

Wolfe sat up a little straighter. Dick was offering an opportunity or a ticket to early retirement. Either way, he planned to emerge a hero. The numbers would tell the story.

"That's right, " Wolfie agreed. "The pressure's on. But I think if you can give me what I need—some overtime and a travel budget, a couple good engineers—and we get those pilot cells operational, we can take five to seven percent out of manufacturing costs. The rest will come. Trust me."

Dick nodded. He knew that Wolfe knew that, for the moment, he had no choice but to trust his old friend. Bufflelunk and Wolfe had come up together through United's ranks. Dick's stint in Marketing had polished his rough edges and caught the founder's attention, while Wolfe's career took a different route—out onto the shop floor and through successively bigger manufacturing operations. Wolfe accumulated in-depth expertise about materials and processes. He knew which tooling suppliers came through and where there was squeeze room in design specifications. His lieutenants loved and respected their leader. Their loyalty took United through all-nighters and dawn patrol meetings. Team spirit. Now, the company needed Wolfe's team more than even they knew.

"Righto," Dick agreed. "I'll get you the support you need. Give me a call on Friday and let me have your full assessment. I'll plan on driving out in two weeks' time after my trip to Germany. It's good to be back working with you, Wolfie."

Dick slapped his old friend's shoulder, opened the door and called for his 3:15 marketing presentation.

4 PM. Bittbeiter sighed, downloaded yet another revised ERP requirements file, and logged off the United system. All his components were under control, either in transit or tucked safely away in Morilla's cage. Blog time!

One click to the blog, six clicks through security, and cobalt blue waves filled the screen.

"WELCOME to Bittbeiter's Blogoshere, an alternative to shaped reality.

You are our first visitor.

Today's question:
Think you're pretty good?
Name one thing that a company can do to shave ten percent off its costs.

Perfect. Punch "send" and seven thousand of the top manufacturing and procurement people in the world would receive three Blog invitations—subtract 20 percent for returned mail, bad filters, dead addresses, and that should yield about 5,000 good messages. Run it again with a new list tomorrow and the next day. Let's see what pops. Check the wire feeds for lead stories, and close up for the night.

Monday morning, 7 AM Status Meeting

Marino couldn't sit down. Their own Wolfie had taken a field promotion, good news for the troops. Gross agreed. "It's great to be wanted! We can make short business of this meeting and get on to the important stuff." Brzezinski stood at the head of the conference table and whipped off a smart salute. Everyone cheered.

"Okay, okay, guys, everybody sit down Let's take it one at a time. I gotta produce an assessment—you know, where we are, quality problems—Kolb, that's you—and shortages—Morilla, that one's yours. You got it, it's all about money. And the ships have to equal the budget this time around. Now I know we've got that under control, even with a few cancellations. "

"You got it!" piped up Brzezinski, eager for a chance to serve the cause.

"But here's the deal." Wolfe's voice dropped, as if he were about to share a long-buried family secret. "You all know, and corporate finally realized, we've got cost issues. We've got to find a way to keep the costs down and show a profit this time around. I know we've had two good kaizen pilots that cut inventory thirty percent and increased throughput about 20 percent. I want to see ten more. Let's move on this."

"Yeah, but …"

"No, John, there's no way out of this one. The target is 15 percent cost down, absolute. No surprises. No excuses."

Meanwhile, Bittbeiter's Blogoshere quietly accumulated posts. By 4 PM, the junior buyer had completed his check of tomorrow's production requirements. Two calls to suppliers, and he was ready for log-on.

Two clicks raised the screen and six clicks through security. "Bingo, looks like we've had some weekend action here," Sean murmured, reaching for a Jolt Cola and a fresh bag of chips. The stream of fresh user entries rolled down his monitor— familiar company names and mystery men among them—Dell, Medrad, the usual consultants plus three anonymous contributors.

His first week as operations director passed quickly for Wolfe. "My guys got shortages under control," he thought. "And no problem with getting customer waivers on partial shipments." He could see the numbers forming up on the screen, 80 percent of ship target and rising. Thanks to Marino and Gross, United had survived the Northwest Plastics meltdown with tooling in place. Parts were expected by the very end of this week. "All systems go!" he wrote on the draft of a report to Dick. This Friday's assessment presentation should be short and sweet. Dick would be pleased to hear pilot cell results—inventories slashed and cell throughput speeded up and smoothed out. Almost 30 percent of the plant workforce had been trained in kaizen

There was only one key summary that would not be out for another month, the cost report. But all indicators pointed to better cost containment, combined with kaizen efficiencies. "You gotta believe, " he thought, "that the pilot savings are real—and they're easily 15 percent or more! But let's see how corporate reacts. Friday, big meeting. Cool."

Dick accelerated out of the parking lot, late for the assessment meeting with Wolfe's staff. All top operations managers would attend. "Now's the time, " he predicted, "when we'll see some real results, no surprises."

Candyman and Brendanne had already reported in from the road with their results—rather, they had e-mailed preliminaries from a dozen suppliers. Time zones intervened, and Blondie seemed increasingly unreachable. Supplier negotiations were encouraging, though. Some three-year contracts came in with five-five-five percent annual reductions. At the back of his neck, just behind his left ear, Dick heard a clock ticking. United Suppliers responded well to personal visits. He might just have to get back on the road.

Get back on the road was right, he thought, as a red Jeep appeared in his rearview mirror. "Haven't I seen that one before?" he thought—something about the front bumper sticker, which seemed to spell out 'Technology rules!' backwards, held his attention two seconds too long.

The turnoff was coming up fast—40, now 35 miles per hour. "Wouldn't do to run the stop sign," he thought as he pushed the brake to the floor.

"Whaaaa?"

" Screee. Thunk."

Dick's head bobbled like a crash test dummy's as his SUV jumped forward. "Where did that come from?" He felt the seat belt cut into his shoulder. A side airbag inflated, pushing his head away from the window. "The red Jeep...."

Bittbeiter's right hand had just downshifted to second, his left locked on a cell phone. A fresh can of Jolt balanced between his thighs. One eye caught cobalt blue movement—laptop slipping!—reach for the keyboard—vehicle dead ahead, coming up fast, contact—too late!.... "Damn, should have strapped the baby in."

Bufflelunk's rear bumper bulged into the Jeep's rusted grille. "Shoot, late for the meeting—" Both drivers sprang from their seats, Bittbeiter still clutching the blue, blinking laptop that continued to flash his newest creation, "Bittbeiter's Blogosphere— Technology Rules!"

"Put the damn computer down, son" Bufflelunk ordered. Bittbeiter had already slipped the guilty cell phone under the seat.

"Sorry, son, I guess I was going a bit over the limit."

"No, I'm sorry sir, multitasking. Don't know what happened. You okay?"

"Sure, sure. Hey, too bad about that grill—quite a vehicle you've got there, bumper sticker and all. So you're a programmer?"

"No sir, junior buyer, electronic components—chips, resistors, capacitors. Hot stuff."

"Is that right? Well, we sure could use some help in that area. Need every nickel we can pull in. Fifteen percent cost down, in fact. That's where I was headed, to the cost reduction meeting, er , assessment meeting."

"Yes, sir." Bittbeiter scrambled to connect the dots. Every anxious e-mail and blog entry pointed to a cost crisis, and here was the confirmation. Corporate was looking for help.

"Uh, sir. I know we've got this Master Kaizen thing going."

"Uh-huh."

"And Blond—ah Brendanne's off trying to squeeze…. renegotiate my contracts.

"Ah, that's right."

"But sir, I wonder if you've ever thought about drawing on the power of the web to come up with some quicker solutions. You know, take a look at what other companies are doing to beat costs…

"Benchmarking? Haven't got time. Too many visits—can't afford to send everybody off to visit Toyota, son! It's gotta happen this quarter!"

"No sir, that's not quite what I meant. Here, take a look at this, sir."

Bittbeiter balanced the laptop on the hood and punched through security to the blog.

"Look, the web allows you to reach thousands of companies overnight, all over the world. We've even got a translator embedded, so we can access anything we want in English, or Portuguese, or even Korean. And people can be anonymous if they want to—think of what that does for suppliers under pressure. You know, sir, our last supplier survey said we are their least favorite customer—wouldn't you like to know why? Wouldn't you like to find out how other companies are finding quick, simple ways to lower their costs? And I'm not talking about the Lopez approach!"

"The Lopez approach? You mean that guy who was at GM?"

"That's the one—tore up contracts, squeezed the suppliers, ate weird stuff, put a lot of little guys out of business. Nearly got vigilanteed. Escaped to Volkswagen."

Bufflelunk's eyes glazed slightly as he watched the

screen scrolling down through messages. "But we've got to bring our costs down. We can't raise prices to find a profit margin—the market won't tolerate increases. We're in a pinch, son."

Security rolled by in a blue and white Ford Explorer, parking lot patrol. Looked like a situation. "Everything all right here? Anything we can do? Tow truck? Ambulance? Crowbar?"

"No, we're fine, officer." Bufflelunk patted back his hair and smiled at the officer. "We've had a little fender-bender and we're exchanging insurance papers. No problem. We'll be on our way in a minute."

"Righto. Looks like you got a couple grand of body work there, buddy."

Bittbeiter groaned and kicked shards of red plastic tail-light into the ditch. Maybe a pry bar would do it.

Chapter 6
The Scribes' Revenge

Marino sketched low riders and chopped rods, Harley tanks and tattoos on his copy of the assessment report, waiting for Wolfie's meeting to hurry up, start and end. Gross entertained the troops with his chopped-finger routine—"that's why they call him Gross," Kathy mumbled as he inserted the stump, all that remained of his index finger after an encounter with an errant steel coil on his first factory job, into his left ear.

The boys were restless. Too many meetings, too much training, no patience. "Aw, come on, I wanna build something," whined Brzezinski.

Of no interest was a single paragraph, three-line entry about Purchasing. Reports in the field from Candyman and Brendanne were sketchy. Wolfe knew they were in contact with suppliers. The results, he believed, would show up long after Accounting prepared an updated profit-and-loss.

Dick's hurried entrance caught Marino's attention. "The big guy's looking flustered. Must be getting pretty hot down in corporate for him to drive out here and play hooky at the plant."

Wolfe took his staff through key manufacturing metrics. The numbers made sense to them—after all, white boards in the aisles tracked shortages, quality issues and shipments. From hour to hour everyone knew when the system flowed well and smoothly, and when obstacles appeared they were instantly visible.

They were on a roll! Wolfe had identified the problems, and his team worked the issues. His guys were in charge now, and they knew how to make the world move. Make things happen. Build product. "If only the suppliers were as good as us, we'd ship every order on time, complete!"

Marino looked up from a finely detailed sketch of flames descending down the side panel of a 1932 Ford roadster. "What the hell is going on in Purchasing, anywho?"

"Updates, updates, folks. Any changes? Good, then that's it. We'll check back in on Monday. Dismissed!"

Dick quietly waited in Wolfe's office. The assessment report looked good—shortages, a timeline of daily ship totals, and Master Kaizen results—all under control. Shortage lists had dropped to a few manageable components, including items stuck on quality hold pending disposition. Jackman was on top of ship schedules, though 60 percent of weekly targets still shipped on Fridays and over the weekend.

Master Kaizen classes continued. Three pilot cells were operational. With each new kaizen event, workers discovered new ways to reduce waste, whether it was excess inventory or wasted human motion. A kaizen team member from Manufacturing Engineering had even calculated the energy savings from cutting electric power to the plant during third shift.

STI continued to emphasize the totality of change required to fully mine United's golden opportunities. The message Dick heard from Deaux was that complete culture change, nothing less, was the only way to deliver United from its rising cost challenges. Training and rewards and recognition would reinforce the Kaizen Master Spirit class lessons.

The door opened and Wolfe's troops marched back to production.

"That was mercifully brief," Dick thought. "Glad I was spared the endless shortage details and supplier problems. Just get on with it, I always say. Do what we pay you guys the big bucks to do, ship product!"

"That kid Bittbeiter work around here, Wolfie?" he asked? Might as well check in with him and see how his Jeep repair bill was coming, settle the damages between themselves, no need to get those nosy insurance companies and their nasty premiums involved. And that blog thing, wonder what had come of that nerdy experiment?

"Who? Oh, you mean Sean? Up in the mezzanine, second door down. Follow the Jolt Cola cans and potato chip bags. I know you'll find him there—he's always there—24/7—weird guy but good with computers. See you next Monday at the club?"

"Sure Wolfe, sure."

Bufflelunk headed up the mezzanine stairs, short of breath and puffing. Good thing it was end of shift—wouldn't want to be seen fraternizing. Just wanted to check it out.

Bittbeiter was bent over a tangle of power cables and tie wraps under his desk. Glowing screens cast a blue tint—oxygen deprivation—on his face. An electronic hum filled the space. Phone chargers dotted the side table and held down thick printouts. Organized chaos, Bufflelunk noted. "Could be a good sign!"

"Knock, knock. Ah, excuse me—"

The junior buyer straightened up—too late—bumping his head on the side of a blinking gray cabinet. "Whatever happened to pocket protector geeks?" Bufflelunk asked himself. Bittbeiter wore the usual United Manufacturing badge, but looped around his neck like Polynesian leis were two memory sticks. No pocket protector in sight.

"Hit the cursor, would you."

"Huh?"

"I said hit the cursor once, would you."

Bufflelunk punched Enter.

"No, no, hit the space bar—the long one—the space bar. Now!"

Too late. Powered down. Argh.

This guy was clearly dangerous around heavy equipment. First the stop sign, then the bumper, and now Bittbeiter's baby, the superfast system he had rigged to capture bits from the Blogosphere. Best get him settled in one place, tie-wrap his hands to his sides, keep his feet on the carpet.

"Well, what can I do for you, sir? Sorry for the mess— just move those printouts. That's it. If you can find a seat, would you like a Jolt Cola?"

Bufflelunk shook his head and settled uneasily into a chair.

"So, how's the Jeep doing?"

"Just fine, sir." He didn't climb those mezzanine stairs to inquire about my busted-up grill, Bittbeiter knew. And the guy was clearly clueless about electronics. So what was this visit about?

Bufflelunk took a couple shallow breaths, his color slowly returning to its normal pink, sighed, rubbed his chin, and tiptoed in. "Son, looks like you've got quite a setup here. What is this blog business, some kind of electronic bulletin board?"

"Close, sir, but actually it's a web-enabled content site—which I control. Kind of my own little printing press. I call it The Scribes' Revenge. Low cost, high reach, instant access. I got a couple buddies in the ozone who've set up blogs for politics and rants. They get some junk responses, but you know, you just delete them and the crazies disappear."

The executive leaned forward, squinting at the junior buyer's biggest screen. A banner materialized, and Bittbeiter scrolled down through yesterday's sports scores and CNN headlines. Ah, there it was, the test Question of the Day.

> We're looking for ideas to cut purchasing spend, real ideas that work without huge SAP-type investments.
> What have you done to cut purchasing costs ten percent or more in your company?

Bingo, up popped three responses, one from a lean consultant—prolific—and two from industry. Bittbeiter highlighted the newest:

Angel L. Mendez
Senior VP-World Wide Manufacturing
Cisco Systems, Inc.

I recently fell in love with a new technique to manage returns, whether it's PDAs or blue jeans. Think about the accounting rules. If you get a return from a customer or from a distributor, even if the package is unopened, you most often can't legally resell it as new. A lot of companies have a 30-day money-back guarantee if customers change their minds. Or the distributor may return goods because of stock rotation or product line end of life. Most companies account for the transaction conservatively and end up taking a cost hit to the "Scrap" account in the month the return arrives, which goes right to the P & L as a COGS debit .

But what if you could resell those perfectly good jeans or PDAs and remonetize the returns? Well, everybody knows about eBay—you can get anything on eBay from cars to cell phones. Or Overstock.com. Use the web to create a forward channel for returned merchandise!

In consumer electronics, returns often represent a single-digit percentage of revenue, about 4-5%. So you take them to a reseller, eliminate all the overhead connected with running a Returns Authorization department and pull some overhead money in as well! Sure, the merchandise needs to be sorted and tested, but you can put it out for sale and recover a fairly sizable amount of original value.

The sales people were worried about cannibalizing original sales, but we learned it's a different customer from one that goes to find a PDA or computer at her favorite electronic store. We started an outlet store on eBay - Palm Outlet Store - and one on Overstock.com to sell refurbished or "not new" returns. We effectively created competition for the inventory between Overstock and our own Palm outlet store. We set it up so that at the end of month we decided who gets the lion's share of the returns inventory this month for resale, based on whoever got the best pricing last month. The reseller makes the sale, keeps a portion and returns the rest to us—bingo, we've monetized about 70-75% of the original product cost!

Bittbeiter straightened up—hmmm, returns, damaged or opened products, that nasty negative line item that marketing bitched about. And here was a three to four percent profit solution! Huh! How 'bout that! And you could empty the DCs of returned product and eliminate the returns authorization department. Yes, Marketing would love this. Cost savings.

"What else you got there, son?"

Sean Bittbeiter warmed to the task. Tonight, he explained, he would post the savings question to a wider audience of bloggers and set the system to e-mail invitations to a bigger circle of supply management, distribution and a few manufacturing pros. His buddies were posting links to Bittbeiter's Blog, and by tomorrow morning there should be more savings ideas posted.

"Stay tuned," he advised.

Chapter 7
Full Disclosure

Dick's one-hour drive back to headquarters took 70 minutes today. The executive found himself drifting off, thinking through the possibilities. He smelled money. The geek was on to something. "Better find a way to keep him on the hook," he thought as he searched for stratagems.

Deus ex machina

A couple guys at ISM (Institute for Supply Management) had been talking about purchasing as something other than a cost center. They called it The Incredible Payback, and claimed that purchasing, that backroom dealmaker, could actually contribute to profitability and growth. And he certainly knew the negative power of the supply base—all the nasty trouble suppliers could stir up with defective product or late deliveries. Still, you wouldn't see a VP of Purchasing ever sitting on United's Board of Directors, so whatever happened, the numbers had to clearly point to a more strategic functional area—his.

With Brendanne and Candyman putting the pressure on suppliers, Wolfie squeezing manufacturing costs, and now this new blogosphere, it should be a snap to come up with 15 percent cost cuts this year. Trouble was, there was no telling who would get there first—best to keep pushing all the options, hitting all the buttons.

Dick's private cell phone buzzed—caller ID declared Blondie calling in. "Arriving plant Friday 4 PM. Dinner? BS." Dick's pacemaker surged as his heart skipped two beats. Wherever she was—and it had become impossible to track that woman down—it was the dead of night. "That means she's busy during daylight putting the pressure on suppliers," he thought. "That's my girl, she can squeeze the hologram right off a credit card. Like the analysts say, she's got traction."

Dick keyed in a discreet reply, "Plant parking lot, 7:30, black pickup." He punched Send and settled in for the rest of the drive.

The Blog seemed a little slow this morning. Bittbeiter checked his virus filters and removed a massive graphics file that was choking main memory. Still, he could have coded a new program in the time it took to raise his morning blog.

Hmmm, ten new posts. Looks like this was going to be a productive day, But first, to e-mail.

> From: Bufflelunk
> To: Bittbeiter, Electronics Procurement
>
> Subject: Systems Review
>
> Sean, will visit plant Friday at 3. Chip pricing up three percent. Need briefing for next quarter budget. Reserve conference room. Call my assistant to confirm.
>
> R Bufflelunk.

No need to respond too quickly. Let him stew, thought Bittbeiter, as he scrolled down through ten new responses to his call for cost savings ideas in the telecom area. United was dotted with competing communications vendors. Every planner and buyer owned one cell, one pager and one land line; there were a few Palms and Blackberries. For travel, the company added an international phone and a calling card. Conference rooms carried extra lines and speaker phones, and fax lines and broadband were ubiquitous.

When Dick Bufflelunk arrived, Bittbeiter was ready. He'd selected the best telecom savings suggestions and compressed them to just the right length for his boss' attention span. The junior buyer planned to feed Bufflelunk a few more rounds of savings suggestions. He wanted out of the plant. A supply manager's title at headquarters would take him two steps closer to running a technology-based global supply chain. And Bufflelunk, even if he thought the blogs were his ticket to fat headquarters retirement, held Bittbeiter's ticket out.

"Wow," thought Bufflelunk, "these guys are incredible. Might be simple for me to take out some easy bucks in the soft areas. They call it low-hanging fruit, but these peaches are way too ripe to squeeze—just pass me that basket!"

"Get me a copy of those posts, would you, son?" Bittbeiter nodded, hit the Print button and forwarded the suggestions to Big Dick's e-mail account.

Friday afternoons in manufacturing can be delightful times to kick back and watch the trucks depart, loaded down with fresh, new customer shipments. Or they can be as anxious as an air traffic control center during bad weather. Either way, by two o'clock Friday, everyone's thinking of tonight's six-pack. By four, the daydream looks more real, and a couple of strung-out faithful decide to start their weekend early with Budweiser bottles out in the parking lot.

Bufflelunk's dreams were not unlike everyone else's, but his credit limit perched thousands of dollars higher. He recalled his last meeting with Blondie at the International Trade Association conference in Singapore He had special plans for their first social encounter back in United Manufacturing territory. So close to home, he would be circumspect about their relationship. Discreet. "Sure," he thought, "Blon—er, Ms. Soufflet and I must debrief the Far Eastern supplier deals that she and Ed Candyman cut. I'll insist that we review her trip reports over dinner. We'll meet in the parking lot, travel in my truck, and I'll get her back to pick up her car long after security has gone for the weekend. "

The last few cars made their way out of the United lot as Bufflelunk emptied his ashtray and loaded a new Diana Krall CD into the Bose. At 7:30 on the dot, Blondie walked through the lobby doors, cellphone at her ear, juggling a briefcase, a black suede shoulder bag, one bottle of Perrier, and a stack of printouts.

Dick rushed to open the passenger door as Blondie looked up, punched in another round of cell phone numbers, and slid into the supertruck's leather bucket seat.

Dinner at Van Dyke's, two towns over, was quiet. Bufflelunk ordered his usual Chivas on the rocks. Blondie drank Tanqueray as she devoured a salad and escargots. They sipped in silence, supplier agreements stacked next to their plates. Brendanne ate quickly. She nodded her approval of the crispy duck. Dick's entrée could have been beef or turkey, he didn't notice. "Gad, that woman can clean a plate faster than a Maytag dishwasher."

"Would you care for dessert, my dear?"

"Mmmph" she responded as she reached for the last yeast roll, layered a quarter-inch of butter on top, took a bite and spread more over the edges.

"The lady will have chocolate torte with crème anglaise, and I'll try the raspberry soufflé." Blondie smiled and emitted a tiny burp. "Ahhh."

The second bottle of Merlot needed emptying. Brendanne raised her glass, waiting for a refill. Dick obliged. "She can drink, too," he thought, pouring himself another. She gulped down the last drops and sat back, glowing.

One hour later in the United parking lot, the couple lingered in Dick's special edition supertruck, an imposing black hulk. The windows were curtained with the couple's moist breath; the heater hummed. Diana Krall, "Live in Paris," crooned "I Love Being Here with You," followed by "Devil May Care." Blondie moaned softly as Dick's thick fingers worked the buttons on her shirt. The cab filled with her warm exhalations. "Faaa," she sighed as Dick carefully shifted his weight across the center console.

"God, I've wanted you since the salad course—here, let me get that out of the way." Dick tugged at Blondie's silk thong, his forehead pressed against the window. Blondie grasped the overhead door strap and shifted her hips. The couple's tangled maneuvers accelerated and sought the steady, pressured rhythm of release. Her right foot buried itself in a pile of discarded garments on the floor—her left foot pressed the dashboard. "Ohhhhh……yahhhhhhh …."

Blondie arched her back. Her left hand grasped the center console stick shift. She pulled the lever back and released four thousand pounds of rugged truck power as she twisted and groaned. The indicator slipped from "Park" to "Neutral" to "Drive," and the 300-horsepower V-8 engaged. The vehicle began to roll—down a slight incline, past the hemlocks and the bronze boulder plaque inscribed "Joe Mason Memorial Picnic Grove," past the barbecue grills and picnic tables. Blondie felt the earth move.

The truck picked up speed as it glided past the United Memorial Softball field "Game Parking" sign. It rolled by the concession stand, the water bubbler and the flagless flagpole. The front bumper nicked a trash can and scraped a bike rack, but still the 22-inch chrome wheels rolled on. Inside the cab, passions and seat belts fully loose, the passengers remained oblivious, twisted into their private embrace.

The truck's front wheels thump-thumped over a concrete parking barrier. Bufflelunk now felt the earth move as an iron park bench raked the oil pan, gouging three-inch furrows into the field. Slowly the truck advanced toward home plate, headed for third, while the couple's frenzied movements accelerated.

Bittbeiter downed his last Jolt Cola, locked his desk, picked up his laptop and headed for the lobby. Just as the glass door closed, he caught the flash of chrome wheels in the moonlight moving across the southwest parking lot. "Buffleunk's truck!"

The junior buyer ran to his Jeep, turned the key, and started after Bufflelunk. Bittbeiter aimed his spotlight toward the trees and shifted up to second, but Bufflelunk's truck had accelerated, left the parking lot and headed through the picnic grove. Bittbeiter's head hit the roof as the Jeep jumped a concrete barrier—thump-thump—and dodged a trash can.

"What's wrong with that guy? Heart attack?"

Bittbeiter punched 911, while 100 feet ahead the black mass plowed through a clump of yews, headed for the outfield. Like David Ortiz at the plate, ninth inning, leaning into the pitch, there was no stopping it now. Bittbeiter reached for his seat belt and his cell phone.

"Lancaster Emergency, Can I help you? Caller, what's your location? Repeat, caller, this is Lancaster Emergency, how can we help you?"

Bufflelunk's vehicle cruised through home plate and rolled toward third. The Jeep wound out as it closed in on the black truck's smoked tail lamps. "Yep, for sure, it's him! Bufflelunk! There's the broken taillight and the creased bumper!"

"I repeat, caller, please identify yourself. What is your location? Describe the emergency."

A low green fence marked the outfield. The truck neatly flattened one section and rolled to a stop against the maintenance dozer. Bittbeiter hit the brakes and aimed his spotlight through the truck cab. He approached the passenger door as a hand wiped away the fog and a familiar face appeared—Bufflelunk himself!

Bittbeiter's flashlight shone on tousled blonde hair as the window rolled down and a faint tang of gin, garlic, sex, sweat and red wine escaped. The occupants scrambled to regain uncompromised positions, and their garments. Bittbeiter aimed the spotlight at his shoes and stood silently by, waiting.

"Er . . . ah . . . you see.   Well, son, we should talk—"

"Yes, sir, that's so. We should talk."

"But the . . . ah . . . transmission . . . we're . . . stuck."

"Sir, turn off the key. Put it in park. I'm going to turn around, and I want you to follow my tracks back up the hill.

Bittbeiter picked up his cell. "Emergency, my apologies. We're okay, and we've got coverage here. Thanks much."

Bufflelunk relaxed as he carefully put the truck in reverse and aimed it back uphill. The Jeep flicked its lights and the black supertruck dutifully followed.

* * *

The junior buyer's phone rang at 7 AM. Caller ID spelled out Bufflelunk.

"Bufflelunk here. Son, I've been looking at the new cost figures, and I want to talk with you about what we're doing in supply management."

"Yes, sir."

"I think there's a future here for you doing strategic planning for critical commodities. I'm creating a new department called Strategic Sourcing, and I want you here as our first commodity specialist. "

"What's that—commodity buying? I'm already doing that…."

"No son, we're talking about consolidating all United purchasing and planning for your commodity—electronics—and maybe a couple others, you know, leveraging the spend."

"Make that commodity manager, and I'll think about it. Tell me the rest."

"The rest?"

"Yeah, the money. What's the compensation?"

Bufflelunk was ready. "The total package, not including bonus, is $225,000. You'll have the same vacation schedule that we all share, three weeks to start. How does that sound, son?"

"I want a new system, and a software budget, and of course tuition reimbursement and time off for my MBA. And stock . . . er, options."

The executive swallowed hard and added smoothly, "Yes, of course. We stand behind your educational plans. Will $350,000 get you into a new system?'

"It's a start. Fax me the offer, and I'll get back to you." Click.

It was the call he'd been waiting for—an invitation to headquarters—new title, new chair, bigger system, bigger future.

Chapter 8
Technology Rules!

> Strange brew, killin' what's inside of you.
> —Eric Clapton

Bittbeiter stashed two boxes of Ramen noodle soup and a case of Jolt Cola under the desk. He was settling in to his new quarters. "This place is made for quiet," he thought. All systems were wireless, and computers booted up at warp speed. The Bittbeiter Blogoshere had bloomed. Each morning the new strategic sourcing manager specializing in electronics and a yet-to-be-decided new commodity group tallied the postings, categorized them and recorded the results.

The blog yielded a strange mix of lofty strategic thoughts—"build customer/supplier partnerships" and "trust is all"—a couple crackpot entries, and some good, usable suggestions from midlevel managers, consultants and some anonymous posters. Some bloggers sent lengthy dissertations describing their successes. Others shot two or three sentences. Many remained anonymous, a tribute to corporate paranoia.

The new job came with a fat budget he'd draw on later. For now, he continued to gather powerful ammunition that he hoped would drive United's next generation supply management strategy. He slapped a new bumper sticker on his laptop— "Technology rules!"—and scanned today's fresh postings.

Implementing just a few of the right suggestions, he thought, would make United's 15 percent cost reduction target easily achievable. Surely the tactics other industry survivors had applied would work here. Bittbeiter was a realist. He knew that executive management needed to see, to touch the results, to vicariously experience what the early adopters had already proven. That's why the words "virtual reality" meant so much to this archgeek turned corporate decision-maker.

Virtual reality, if he presented it correctly, would take the pain and risk out of what Bufflelunk preached as complete culture change. Seeing is believing, they said, and Bittbeiter planned to gradually convince the doubting Thomases of technology tools' power to affect reality.

First off, Bittbeiter punched a new commodity segment into the blog—MRO, those soft expenditures from Maintenance and Repair Operations. MRO and other soft costs like travel, health benefits, public relations, printing and copying, legal and even cafeteria management, were all areas in which United had no special expertise. Deals were scattered across the corporation—anybody and everybody was a decision-maker, hence the accumulation of assorted suppliers. But Bittbeiter remembered hearing a webcast by former IBM CPO Gene Richter, who proved that consolidation—not maverick buying —and strategic sourcing leverage held the key to big gains that could carry the company into its next, more difficult cost reduction area. In fact, starting a cost reduction campaign with MRO's low-hanging fruit was a great way to build momentum. Step by step, Bittbeiter knew the answer to the cost challenge was on his computer. Good, proven ideas arrived daily in his Blogosphere from guys who'd been there and done it. But first, he'd have to accumulate more ideas and sell them. And to sell them he'd have to get by Bufflelunk.

Let the numbers speak
–Dorian Shainen, Shewhart Award winner

Bittbeiter's e-mail flashed a summons to Bufflelunk's office. Time to brief Dick for his central staff meeting. A couple juicy suggestions would do it . He scanned the postings.

Question: How can companies save 10% on their soft costs?

Mike Frederickson
EVP
KineticWorks
Mike.fredrickson@kineticworks.com
"Your one source for telecom management."

Telecom!
Do you know how much you are spending on local, LD, pagers, wireless, and other network-related expenses? Most small to medium sized organizations do not manage the full life cycle of telecom expenses and services because they do not have the tools, resources and expertise to keep up with the ever-changing telecom industry. Without addressing each phase of the life cycle each and every month, companies can be over-spending by as much as 30%. By outsourcing your telecom expense management, you can save up to 30% your first year.

If you are not auditing your bills every month, you could be throwing money away—7-10% of your spend could be in error!

The first step to managing telecom is to organize all your telecom inventory and eliminate all the waste. It is important to understand that even if the item was canceled, your company may still get billed for it.

Next, review all contracts with all services, and prepare a competitive analysis of what's in the marketplace. You may be able to renegotiate with existing carriers or get a new carrier for 10-15% less.

The key to purchasing the correct service is to work with an expert who has relationships with all providers. Voice, data, wire-less—it's all a commodity these days, which makes purchasing decisions very difficult. For example: In major markets today, there are over 10 local providers to choose from. 7-8 years ago there was only one!

The changeover to new carriers is a critical implementation. We take away the hassle by managing the conversion process. We use our own software to track all telecom accounts and the inventory changes throughout the life cycle. We also monitor and negotiate contracts on the customer's behalf to capture lower

"Hmm…. yes…. excellent." As Bufflelunk scrolled

lower costs as they drop, usually 2 times during a typical 3-year contract term. That means we are talking about 15% savings the first year; the next year could be 5-10%

Here's another way to uncover savings. When you find a lot of errors, it's time to do an historical audit. We go back about 3 years and collect all the overcharges. Let's say you spend $10,000 per month and you are overcharged by 10%. That's $1,000 per month, times 36 months, or $36,000 we could recover—without lawyers!

It works with big and small companies. We've worked with 10-employee operations that spend $1,500 per month; we've saved them $500. They pay based on a percentage of the savings. The biggest company we've implemented was 500 employees with $100,000 total monthly expense.

There are other critical telecom areas such as equipment selection and acquisition, and disaster recovery solutions which we also help manage for our clients.

Sam Santosuosso
Director, Supply Chain Management
Axcelis Technologies, Inc.
Beverly, Mass. 01915
Samuel.Santosuosso@axcelis.com

Last year we auctioned a "lot" of clean room supplies annual requirements @ $350K spend and saved about 17%. Here are my two recommendations:

Develop a cost out strategy for buys that are easy to define, highly competitive and have multiple possible suppliers (i.e., direct materials such as simple machined parts or MRO supplies such as clean room supplies.

Incorporate an e-auction process and tool that is inexpensive and easy to use.

Bill Frankel
Managing Partner
Ascher Group, LLC
Phone (303) 285-9221
Fax (720) 554-7988
bfrankel@theaschergroup.com
www.theaschergroup.com

Printing and copying costs!

We saved Insurance Auto Auctions, Inc. $6.6M. Their administrative support costs had grown faster than the company. With over 80 locations, nearly 1,000 employees and an annual location growth rate of 12%, they were accumulating costs and systems that did not add value.

We did an analysis of each area, designed new systems, took these areas out to bid, managed the implementation and continue to manage procurement. The results were dramatic—overall cost savings of 39%, all while upgrading technology and services. The dropdown to corporate America is 2-5% for the average company spending on this group of products.

More results for Insurance Auto Auctions—

Copiers/faxes—59% cost savings over previous contract, 97% of copier fleet upgraded, consolidated equipment to coterminous contract.

Mail machines—26% cost savings over previous contract, fleet upgraded to new digital technology, consolidated fleet

Overnight shipping—26% rate cost savings, 21% cost savings from review of shipping methods, 13% cost savings from overcharges

Office supplies—cost savings of 22% from current suppliers, consolidation of more than 500 vendors into one national supplier.

The scope was: 146 copiers, 105 faxes, 46 mail machines off contract, overnight shipping for 80 locations, office supplies.

Here's how we did it:

We reviewed current systems and equipment, developed Requests For Quotes, helped evaluate and compare bids; made recommendations. We negotiated the contract and implemented the new systems. We continue to audit bills and deal with vendors and procurement.

Want to know how to save 10% right away? Tell them you

have a consultant involved! For example, Insurance Auto Auctions had a long-standing contract with Xerox . In fact, the agreement was so old that no original contract could be found! We spent three months doing discovery to find out what equipment was in the field in 78 locations against what they really needed. The industry tends to "oversize" people— you end up buying a Ferrari to deliver pizzas. Sure, you'll get it done faster, but you won't make a profit.

Second, look beyond current needs. We found out volumes were going to increase out at the branches. That led us to a list of vendors that could meet all the requirements; next we developed a specific equipment configuration for each branch. THEN we took it to bid. That's when to include special requirements, such as when to replace the unit. The RFP is important because it enables apples to apples comparisons across vendors.

On Federal Express we saved 25% by reviewing overnight shipments, changing from priority overnight to second and third day and ground. Not every package has to go priority overnight!

Audit accounts payable—We discovered 13% overcharges from one shipping provider. The rates were entered incorrectly, and so we got $13,000 back.

For Monarch Beverage we found 4% cost savings by solving two printer uptime issues.

Preventive maintenance—Many providers use a "break and fix" approach, but preventive maintenance calls save money and productivity. That's why you should review maintenance records.

Service vs. savings—The law offices of McKenna, Long and Aldrich achieved 22% cost savings on office products when our audit revealed $12,000 of overcharges between two office product centers. After we took the business out to bid, we decided not to go with lowest price. We chose second-lowest price to get the right service level. We continue to monitor this commodity. You almost need to take them out to bid every two to three years to stay on top of paper pricing and market shifts.

Don't consider copier or Fed Express something you are just going to get ripped off on, and don't assume your relationship with these vendors is so good that they won't rip you off. They will. It's shocking. Don't take it for granted, even if you do it once per year. I did a postmortem on bids for the Archdiocese of Seattle and discovered they weren't getting the nonprofit or church pricing. We actually had to go back and beat down the vendors 30% to get them to honor the national church pricing. If they will rip off a church, they will definitely rip off anybody!

through Bittbeiter's Blog, like a pig rooting for truffles, he unearthed the biggies. He would tuck away a few gems for next year's budget work-up. He needed cost reductions now, and though telecom and MRO looked like interesting areas, there was not a central buying department at United to run a single leveraged sourcing initiative. It made much more sense, and better politics, to go with lean manufacturing cost savings and supplier cost cuts. The company had left its buying to the plants, and none of the division managers wanted to surrender their million-dollar buying power. Yes, the cuts would have to come from Manufacturing and the suppliers.

"The cost reductions would," he assured the directors, "be realized by total kaizen culture change and ongoing contract negotiations with United's vast global supply base." No need to explain further, just show me the money, he chuckled, as he punched projected savings numbers.

"That'll be all, son. Excellent work. Thanks." Next, he turned to his Kaizen Kulture Change Report from Wolfe. "Good ol' Wolfie, " he sighed, "a real team player." Wolfe's numbers reported incredible results.

Kaizen results:

35 % of all employees trained in basic Kaizen Master Methods
4 pilot cells operational
Inventory savings—50%
Floorspace savings—40%
Productivity—up 50%
Quality—15%
Shipments—2% above target
Aged backlog—5.5 weeks

How could aged backlog increase at the same time

shipments rose? Oh well, must be some unevenness in Jackman's schedules. But how about those savings in inventory and floorspace! I'll have to call Deaux and share the good news! And with productivity up 50 percent, that will of course free up workers for big savings in direct labor. Overall, I think we're looking at projected 25 percent reduction in cost of goods sold, well above target! We'll be heroes! Pile that on top of the supplier price cuts flowing in from Blondie and Candyman, and I've got the formula for United's continued market dominance. Who said China is the only cheap place to manufacture?

Planes and boats and trains

More new savings ideas bubbled up in the Blog. Out at the perimeter of the extended enterprise, Bittbeiter noticed some activity in the far-flung area of Transportation, Logistics and Distribution—Jackman's empire. Although Transportation and Logistics were unglamorous areas rumored to be populated by beaned-up, red-eyed truckers, guys whose career options ranked below Manufacturing, Bittbeiter knew it was an expensive area to operate. Some companies spent 20 percent of their budgets on packaging and shipping. And everyone accepted the critical service the folks at the end of the line continued to deliver under duress. This might also be a gold mine of opportunity.

"I wonder how the Mr. Universe runner-up is doing back at the plant."

Bittbeiter had good reason to think twice about Logistics' costs because he had observed a constant flow of superhot priority shipments for his electronics orders. There was a lot of money in packaging materials—all sizes and varieties, and lots of it. Used packing material from inbound supplier shipments, as well as outbound customer orders, stacked six feet high down at the docks. During peak times Jackman set up a mini assembly line to move packing and documentation.

There had to be a better way, a different approach to running product in and out of the plant that would not accumulate premium freight charges and packaging expense. A way that would not leave workers exhausted at the end of the quarter.

Shipping might be a hard area to tackle; in fact he envied Jackman's shipping empire. Everyone respected the pace at which Jack's department worked, and the absolute leverage the weightlifter held over all product managers. It would be tough to make any changes. Nothing short of a nuclear blast could level plant production schedules and eliminate priority shipments.

But perhaps there was another way to bring order into the whole packing and shipping equation while reducing costs. Kathy Parmenter, Jackman's right-hand man, ran the operation with a doggedness and giddy approach to hourly crises that kept events from exploding. She might make a valuable commodity specialist. After all, the Blog was telling him that he would need someone experienced in transportation and logistics, with a bigger view to strategic targets, new blood.

Question: How can companies save 10% on their transportation, logistics and distribution?

Elijah Ray, past president of CSCMP and Senior VP of customer solutions for Uti Integrated Logistics

One factor that impacts financial metrics is order cycle time, or the amount of time it takes for an order to work its way through the network. A complex distribution network like Wal-Mart's, for example, involves order processing, import facilities, de-consolidation and processing to regional centers and final shipment to the store.

These four or five steps must each be tracked and well managed because days in inventory cost money, a critical business metric. In some companies, if you can take just one day out of inventory, you can save millions. Look at velocity through the pipeline as well as demand planning to control the flows.

Logistics are almost 10% of our GDP, and transportation is the biggest piece. Does it make sense to ship goods to China for assembly, and then to bring them back and deconsolidate and ship them, when we can cut logistics costs right here?

Raul Fernandez
VP of Technology and Innovation
Chiquita Fresh North America
rfernandez@chiquita.com
Raul can also be reached at
'breakthoughsolutions@gmail.com'

Packaging!

We are in the food business, and we have located our R & D group that creates our corrugated and plastic packaging ideas, right next to our growing areas. It allows us to go from concept to execution very quickly. Our "in market" teams can quickly transfer an identified unmet customer need to the team that can find and execute the right solution.

"Fail early, fail cheap."

There is a lot of brainstorming and trial and error—It's one thing to know the theory, but you have to test it in the real world. "Fail early, fail cheap" allows you to quickly test and evaluate concepts, as much and as quickly as possible to sort the brainstorms with potential from the no-go's.

For instance, we make our own boxes. We buy our own roll stock. By designing and making boxes ourselves, we reduced the number of different paper types from 27 to 6. That allowed us huge savings—we had used many different widths and thicknesses—but by redesigning some of the packages, we discovered that we could use the same paper for different boxes and take advantage of scale to obtain better pricing when purchasing.

Paul Sheldon@SheldonWorks.com
Teaming with Companies to Locate, Originate and Exploit
Strategic Technology
voice: 262-241-9025   fax: 262-241-4837
www.sheldonworks.com

I've been working on optimizing packaging and shipment of foods internationally. Bananas, for example, have to be shipped at just the right temperature, which means special trucks and boats. Because of the specificity of the shipping requirements, it's important to optimize both the packaging and the mode. We know that China will be importing more food from the West, so it's crucial for us and other growing areas to figure out the best and most cost effective ways to ship into new markets.

Diana Twede
Assoc. Professor, School of Packaging, Michigan State University
twede@msu.edu

Packaging!
Those poor little packages can do an awful lot for you. You can cut transportation costs in half if you make the package half the size. We have an alumnus at HP, Kevin Howard, responsible for postponement on packaging of printers—$2 million per month savings—not from customization or inventory reduction, but mostly because he cut the cost of transportation in half. They shipped printers all over the world, mostly from Vancouver, Washington, with no packaging.

So here's how it went. It started with customerization. The printers were packed in boxes in Vancouver. If a printer was going to France, it would be boxed with a different power cord and a different manual and language. Sometimes they would have the wrong number of French printers in the wrong place—they could not predict demand well enough, were always tearing apart and repacking. That's where Kevin started. He came up with a box you could customerize and then he went beyond that. You could ship into a DC in Europe, for instance, and then ship the order out from there, customerize the label, manual, etc., for France or Germany or Poland.

There was an article in HBR about postponement, but what the article didn't talk about was that by shipping without the box and without cushioning—the only reason you put cushioning around the printer is to protect it from the danger of drop damage from waist-high loading on the dock—since they are shipping to the foreign DC in pallet-load quantities, they don't need it. The pallet won't be dropped because it's a bulk pack. Once the bulk pack reaches the DC, they customerize and ship it out as a onesie.

Think how much volume the polystyrene foam cushion takes. Just by getting rid of the cushion, the bulk pack can hold twice as many bare naked printers as when in the box. Kevin used foam sheets and stretch wrap, so the air containers could take twice as many. So what happens when you ship twice as many printers in the same space? You cut transportation costs—$2 million a month including all the extra packaging cardboard, foam, labor in foreign countries. Plus you save on inventory because you're shipping a generic printer, instead of one printer for France, one for Germany, one for Poland. But the biggest savings was the cube savings, and that's a hard message to convey.

We have computer programs that help figure out pallet stacking—you program the shipping container dimensions, and the software tells you what patterns on the pallet will best utilize the space. One package is called CAPE, a competing one is TOPS. The nice thing about them is they start with the shipping container size and give the best pattern, but they also can redesign the shipping container so it better fits on the pallet. If you make shampoo or Rice Krispies, you could figure out the best size for the box . Just by changing the box by a couple millimeters, more goes on the pallet, therefore transportation costs drop.

Remember, transportation over the road either cubes or weighs out. There is a weight limit, usually 40K pounds per trailer. If you are shipping beer in glass bottles, you can never fill up the trucks—it would weigh too much. In that case your packaging strategy is to change the weight. If it cubes out, you have to figure out how to reduce the cube. If you have beer in plastic vs. glass bottles, you'll get more bottles into the truck! When people have looked at this, they've seen they could change the weight of the glass also.

So this is another example of how to reduce transportation costs—pallets take space, and everybody is trying to figure out how to get the pallet out of the ocean container but still handle the material mechanically, not hand-load. HP has done a lot with looking at slip sheets, board under load, special lift truck—not forks—which reduces the amount of cube and still is mechanical. Saves money.

*

William E. Miller
President, Crosscut Group, Inc.
WMiller@CrosscutGroup.com
Naperville - Robbinsville - Strongsville
(630) 240-7486 mobile
(630) 904-1322 office

Big transportation savings!

Take a look at hardcore transportation stuff. There are huge competitive pressures like fuel prices and federal motor carrier regulations. Plus we have more imports than ever. With all this going on, there frequently is a lack of attention to transportation.

We go in and help without disrupting priorities. There are some simple things you can do to improve.

Nine out of ten shippers need to give consideration to the mode and sub-mode of transportation they are using. For example, you've got a DC in Chicago serving customers in California, Colorado, and so forth. and you are using overnight service, two-day team driver premium transportation. Now that is extraordinarily expensive, and 98 out of 100 times it is not needed—it usually masks other problems. You have to step up to it and question the mode you are using. Whether you are using full truck or LTL, have you considered intermodal? In particular with drug companies, we ask, "Why are you using so much air freight?" There is no reason why drugs can't go on an equally secure but more effective sub mode—not premium, but regular dry van service. And even if we're using specialized equipment like refrigerator or tanks, we still need to question why normal single driver service wouldn't suffice, instead of the premium for two drivers. I call the mode selection issue more of a transportation strategy decision, not something that you handle tactically.

The tactical end of this gets down into where we want to bridge from strategic to tactical once I have determined what the true requirements are and what offerings will satisfy. Every small company can do a simple stratification of their shipping and really uncover which items require premium shipping.

Here's an extreme example - aluminum motor castings. The company planned to use rail, loading into box cars and shipping via rail from 750-1500 miles. That's a relatively inexpensive mode, but combination of service uncertainty—does it take a week or ten days? You are never sure in transit—coupled with a lack of understanding of what the client really needs, starts driving the decision to ship things via truck. So now transportation costs just went up 30-40%. But it gets worse. They're still having problems and still missing customer commitments, so they go to premium truck and add another 25% cost. The root of the problem was their own lack of sales and operations planning.

We helped them segment the business and save money. They weren't ready to reengineer sales and ops planning, but it was possible to segment. We put some shipments on the rail, which took cost out. We put some in normal truck mode, and in this way only a little piece went premium, 10-15 %, instead of 90%! So the strategy was, break it down and keep at it.

It's not that complex—there are just two things to do. We don't want to make it too difficult to execute:

1. Simple stratification
2. Gain the knowledge of what the transportation market can do for you. Educate yourself about the capabilities of modes and carriers.

Here's another opportunity area—

Nobody manages inbound freight. The auto companies say they do with just-in-time and kanban, but they are just sort of managing it. Take seats, a great B-school example. Let's say I buy my seats from Lear; they are manufactured in Mexico and shipped to Tennessee, where there is a consolidation center. They do really good things in between the consolidation center and plant - everything appears to be just in time, and for the most part, it all works well. But what's not being managed and where cost is not well controlled, is what's going on inside Lear feeding that consolidation center. So we are extending the view of the supply chain; working with suppliers is key.

Some of it depends on what can potentially be done—if you are really big and powerful, you have more leverage in the freight market than your supplier does, so you need to take advantage of that. You don't want product shipped to you prepaid, and if you do it that way, then insist upon working with the supplier to make that decision who it will be shipped on. A couple years ago companies used prepaid inbound to collect conversion—that means the receiver of the shipment is now responsible for the freight. We used to do that because we were always working with really big companies who had a lot of clout and could get better pricing than any of their suppliers. The other reason is to gain control—control the scheduling, the level of service, etc., carrier selection. Either on the sourcing process, or on the tactical basis, we can design the routing guide, not the supplier. Big companies can do this, but frequently they don't.

We make part of procurement strategy to make the call on delivery . If I don't control it and specify exactly, at least I will influence the decision that my supplier is making. We call it an influence model. BP Chemicals was trying to incorporate in their procurement contract that they will specify delivery mode. The benefit shows up in being able to actually negotiate the normal delivery charge for the trucks, the transportation fee on the sticker, not a standard one size fits all. You want to make certain, on the price of a tractor, that it's only 1% max.

So the influence model is the way to do it. For smaller companies the influence model makes sense. If you have what you believe are good contracts with outbound carriers, use them for inbound. Nearly all dry van carriers—JBHunt, Schneider—can come in, unload and live load, or they will do a drop trailer program if you have any scale at all. They will usually prime the pump with an empty trailer, then come with an inbound load, drop it at the dock, and you unload at your leisure. The drop trailer program is embedded in the overall freight price; they'll give you one empty for every ten; for paper companies, you might have 50-100 dropped trailers to get the ball rolling.

Here's the deal: if you are any where near balance, you should not have a charge, because you are helping the trucker get better utilization of drivers, trailer and tractors. But if it's 100% unbalanced, you'll need one empty for every load out. Then it will come out to a negotiated issue that will depend on the market and where you are. If you are in a location of surplus, they will do it for nothing, they want your business, or if you are in West Texas where trailers are scarce, you will have to look at it. This approach can save you a bunch of money. For example, if you are live-loading, you have the cost for the regular shipment, $1,000 plus live loading accessorial fee based on driver cost plus about $25-30 per hour. So the solution is to take that off and spend it on a drop trailer or put it in your pocket. The drop trailer might be free, or there might be a $5, $10, or $15 fee, depending on the market and location.

Small companies are real abusers of live loading, because it doesn't dawn on them there could be another way. Their vision is limited, and they don't have time to be looking out there. If the carrier doesn't offer it to them—and a carrier won't unless it's beneficial to them—they won't know they can save money this way.

Bulk Shipping, another opportunity area.

Bulk Shipping has some of its own characteristics, asset considerations that absolutely have to be part of the decision-making process, and for small and medium sized companies, they frequently aren't figured in. If you are Exxon Mobil, you track utilization that ships plastic in and manage the heck out of it. If you are a little guy, you probably aren't managing and don't know you can. The first step here is take a long, hard look at capacity, service requirements and rates for different service levels. You've got to play that, modulate it to your best advantage. Frequently, the decision becomes, can I finance more equipment, or should I pay a higher rate to get the reliability and speed?

Those are the biggest and easiest things you can do. As you step beyond that to pipeline visibility management, the focus could be either outbound or inbound. For inbound as well as outbound, big or small bulk, discrete, you have to consider your infrastructure, your people, your shipping and receiving process, your level or lack of technology —all of that—and the performance of those things vs. what truly are the requirements. Ask, what is my supply chain strategy, how do we do things, what are we trying to accomplish. Match what I have vs. what's there, and that points to what I need to focus on and which ideas. Do a gap analysis of your transportation business to find opportunities. I created something like that at Accenture—I prefer to do an assessment first.

One of the best examples is the old Mobil Oil. They don't exist anymore. They blamed the railroads for all their bulk shipping problems. They were shipping base stocks from one place to another, then manufacturing products. The base stocks, large volumes, all moved by rail, and the fact that the manufacturing plants would run out was always the railroad's fault. It was a blanket excuse, everything is the railroad's fault.

But let's map this out. Forty percent of all activity and 70% of the time is under Mobil's control, inside their gate. They are the ones sitting on cars and not loading them, taking cars in and not unloading them, and the reason for that is that they didn't know what to do. The refinery did the best they could, which might be the bare minimum; there were people trained to load and people trained to submit the proper paperwork, although this continues to be one of the big issues in rail shipping.

But they just don't know the peculiarities about the mode; it's not something they think about. "We are refining and I don't have to worry about that" is what you'll hear. Eventually the rail cars escape the refinery, it takes about a week from the Gulf Coast to Chicago. They arrive and they want to deliver to the plant, but the plant is filled. So the railroad has to stop, make some calls, wait. It's the same ballet every time, like pulling teeth to figure out what has to be done, and from the receiving plant, it's simple—take my empties and bring in my loads and arrange them this way.

So how does the railroad know everything you want them to know? In the old Mobil Oil nobody told them, and they didn't know how to anyway. It was a broken process with a broken information flow. Corporate is thinking, "Hey, the railroads have everything screwed up," when in fact we fixed the whole thing internally. We dedicated some management to rail shipping. This takes focus and knowledge and training. Someone who isn't fully trained in shipping might not be able to do it. The benefit was in asset utilization. We could take hundreds of rail cars out of the fleet. For just one rail car, the minimum expense was $80,000 per year. When there are hundreds, this can save millions.

* * *

In a short time Central Strategic Sourcing had expanded to two members—Sean covering electronics and Kathy on distribution and logistics. That left millions of dollars yet unconsolidated, in packaging, plastics, travel, fuel, computers, employment services.

"Let's start small," Sean thought. "We need to grow consistently—no surprises." For every million dollars saved, we'll pick up one more commodity manager. Technology rules!"

Bittbeiter shut off the lights, grabbed his keys and headed toward the stairs. The Blog happily hummed, working hard overnight, a thousand scribes converted to electronic impulses. Ones and zeros filled the universe.

Chapter 9
The Basics

Dick Bufflelunk, affectionately called RB by some of the directors and BS by others, strode into the directors' budget meeting, armed with numbers showing growing cost reduction success in two areas.

Chairman Bob Crain opened the meeting with a snapshot of United's position—cash balance unchanged, some slippage in market share, new products in the pipeline, but what was happening with Manufacturing?

Bufflelunk was ready. He clicked on PowerPoint slide number one and began to tell the Kaizen Kulture Change story.

"When we started on this campaign just a few months back, we didn't really know what we were getting into."

"No kidding," Marketing VP Henry Ross shot back. "That's why you guys wear the white socks—so we can see where you're all at!"

"Right , Henry, it's Manufacturing that's going to save your pretty tails . . . again. We've tackled the cost reduction targets on two fronts—Manufacturing and the supply base. And the results are unbelievable."

"Sure, sure BS, get to the numbers! Show me the money," someone laughed as Bufflelunk pointed his laser at slide number one, "Manufacturing Cost Savings:"

Manufacturing costs:
Before Kaizen Kulture Change	$165M
After Kaizen Kulture Change,	
Projected Mfg. Costs	$132M
Projected savings	$ 33M

"Whoa! That's way, more than 15 percent savings!"

"That's right," Bufflelunk confirmed. "My guys don't know when to let up. I told them 15 percent cost down would do it, but they overreacted, got religion on this lean stuff, and now they're projecting in excess of 20 percent savings. Not bad for beginners, huh?"

For once, the room was silent, the only sound a low hum from the projector. Bufflelunk continued.

"Hold on! There's more! We've got a second source of savings—the suppliers."

No one moved. Purchasing was a back-room operation that everyone trusted Bufflelunk's Operations guys would handle. Who wanted to deal with those problem suppliers? No need to get into the messy details, they thought. Nevertheless, BS's pointer relentlessly zeroed in on one more number, purchased price cost reductions.

"Now," he began, "nobody wants to disrupt supply lines, but we know that we have a few fat and happy suppliers. And they're long overdue to show a little cooperation. That's why I've put my best people out on the road to renegotiate contracts and reel in purchased parts savings. It's early in the game, but we're beginning to get some results."

Andy Benson, United's corporate accounting director, nudged Ross, the Marketing VP. "See?" he whispered, "What did I tell you? They're going after the suppliers! It's The Big Squeeze."

Ross' smile widened as he nudged back, "About time!"

Bufflelunk's second slide contained only four numbers:

Current purchased costs	$ 275M
Reductions to date from three suppliers	$ 2.75M
Additional projected annual savings	$13.75M
Projected Purchased Cost Total	$258.5M

"We've got our best people pushing both envelopes,"

he intoned. "Deaux says we're among his top ten cost reduction clients. I figure if we keep it up, my division will come up with enough savings to make bonus AND build that new plant down the road. And that's just the first year!"

BS closed the PowerPoint file and sat down to stunned silence—no need to show the final slide—Blog cost reduction recommendations. "It's always good to have a back-up. And this is one pretty powerful Plan B," he thought.

Kathy Parmenter's day lengthened to 12 hours as she tallied up the morning's blog entries. She felt a certain familiar pressure just behind her left ear, and her stomach flipped a few times as the pages rolled on—responses from managers in the UK, a few in Europe, as well as dozens of e-mails from North America. It was an avalanche, and it would take days to dig out. Time pressure was unyielding. The sooner she got these ideas summarized and categorized, the faster her new career would accelerate.

"Well," she thought, "being at headquarters working a keyboard sure beats dodging Jackman and his endless trucker jokes. It's about time my career showed real mortgage potential." Kathy had her eye on a piece of riverfront property. Her new boss, Sean Bittbeiter, seemed to be doing quite well at United, probably because he's a nerd, she thought, but whatever. If sitting at a desk and reading all day paid as well as she hoped, she planned to give Evelyn Wood Speed Reading a call.

Bittbeiter flew in, mumbling about numbers and projections. "Kathy, can you give me an update on savings suggestions from the Blog as of this morning?"

"Sure, Sean, We've got 47 MRO postings, some repeats and continuations, not counting two spammers. Looks like we're easily talking 20 to 30 percent reductions on telecom. The other percentages are pretty good, and I haven't even tackled your basic strategic sourcing gambits. Wanna hear about trucking?"

"You got it. "

"Okay, as of this morning we got 51 various responses in transportation and logistics. Of course, that includes packaging and some random coordination suggestions, but it's solid. And let me tell you, as a former serf in Jackman's shipping empire, the money spent on premium delivery services is huge—huge enough to buy me a couple acres on Wyman's Pond, or at least to clear the land."

Bittbeiter knew she wasn't exaggerating. But management had no patience for more than three PowerPoints, or maybe four pages of Executive Summary max. When it was time, he wanted to be ready with a succinct summary, two pages, no more. He would cite named corporate success stories for each commodity category, and lay out the real savings numbers. Certified.

"Looks like we're going to need more help," he said, as he punched in Bufflelunk's private cell phone number. Kathy grinned.

Bufflelunk's secret cell phone vibrated, signaling a call from one of only four people who had this confidential number—Blondie, Bittbeiter, RB's wife MJ, and his assistant Lynne. It was an outside call, probably Bittbeiter checking in.

"Bittbeiter here. How did the directors' meeting go?"

"Just fine, Sean. We're on board for huge cost reductions, starting with shop-floor kaizen pilot projects. And of course our big purchasing initiative to squeeze…. uh, revisit supplier contracts. But you've called at a bad time, I'm off to another meeting— can't talk. Call me tomorrow."

"Hold on there, RB. We've got a deal, remember? I'll build the corporate sourcing team, starting with my Blog, but I need more heads—we're avalanched here with cost savings ideas. It's just too much for the two of us to handle. Speaking of too much to handle, how's Blondie? Haven't seen much of her around the cafeteria since we ran into each other that night on the ball field."

Bufflelunk knew where Bittbeiter was going with this. There was no need to say more.

"All right, Sean, I got your point. What do you need, one, two more commodity managers?"

"Four should just about do it for now, RB. And when you see Ms. Soufflet, give her my regards." Click.

The call left Bufflelunk with a tightening in his chest, a familiar feeling of pressure below the sternum, as if someone had wrapped thick bungee cords around his ribs. He was being squeezed.

The next call he received tightened the bungees even more. Wolfe was on line one. It was a call Buffelunk would replay, word-for-word, at three in the morning.

"Er, RB, thought I'd give you a heads-up."

"Yes, Wolfe, what's cookin'? We talked about your Kaizen Kulture Change numbers at the directors' meeting this morning. Everyone was floored with the gains—"

"That's why I called. We're hearing from Kantargis out in Field Service that something's causing big field failure rates. We've got most of last month's shipments DOA and this month is still in the pipeline. I have a feeling about this one—"

"What do you mean you've got a feeling? Feelings don't count for much around here, Wolfe. You know the drill. Marketing wants happy customers, and even with a few quality problems, you've always been able to come up with the goods. Send a tech out , for chrissakes!"

'You know," said Wolfe, "we tried that. Gross took a plane to the coast yesterday, and he's got a bunch of disassembled units in his hotel room. Something about capacitors. I'll let you know as soon as we know more, but it don't look good. Two single source suppliers have shipped partial orders, we've got rejects in the other one, and the schedules are all shot to hell. It ain't pretty."

"Now see here, Wolfie. Calm down. We've got to make shipments. If we don't play, they won't pay. And Marketing won't accept low quality. You've got to fix it and fix it fast."

"I've got my best guys on it. We're searching for replacements, and we're going to have to run assembly over the weekend. You'd better drop some overtime money back into my budget. I'm telling you, these suppliers ain't comin' through for us. What the hell is going on down in Purchasing?"

Bufflelunk groaned and fell back on his pillow. The house was quiet. No light shone through tightly curtained windows. His throat constricted as he tried to swallow. He needed more air. Wolfe had asked exactly this question, just what the heck was going on in Purchasing? Well, at least the pilot cells were a glorious success. . . .

Chapter 10
All the King's Horses and All the King's Men

It was nine in the morning a few months later. The newly assembled strategic sourcing commodity team gathered around Kathy Parmenter's desk as she rolled through a blog update. Her eyes were tired and red. She was looking for a quick way to dig through the avalanche of savings suggestions.

"Listen, guys, we've got some heavy lifting to do. Sean needs us to pull together a few million dollars of cost savings. He says if we stick with what we've got, that ought to do it. And since we've got clearance to take over the plants' buying—for the entire corporation—just say the word." A cheer erupted from the group. They knew that by finally consolidating United's spend with a few good suppliers, they'd bring in the bucks. "We've looked at MRO—that's you, Dave—and Transportation and Logistics, and Packaging—my area—plus electronics—for now that's Sean. Chris and Hiroshi, we'll need your cost savings estimates today. No problem, right?"

"Sure."

"Yeah."

"Piece of cake."

"Whaa?" Hiroshi was a little slower on the uptake, but he always came through.

The team settled into the war room, a single gray cubicle whose walls they'd pushed out to accommodate Bittbeiter's five commodity specialists and their laptops. They were looking at a wide and scattered rolling landscape of incredible proportions, all over the world. Every day they saw market prices of basic commodities shift as new suppliers surfaced. It was an uneven perspective, dotted with negotiated contract costs, underlaid with true costs for things like plastics, fuel, phones. And somewhere between the market and the base cost, Bitbeiter's commodity specialists were digging in, excavating until they hit the solid substrate.

Later that afternoon, after Bittbeiter's blog scans were nearly complete, a corporate e-mail announcement arrived. Several key words caught his attention— accounting irregularities, temporary leave, kaizen cost savings—corporate code for tectonic movements down in the executive offices. He downloaded the full text and began to read the memo aloud as the commodity team members rolled their chairs over to his corner to listen:

United Manufacturing

To: All United Manufacturing Employees
From: Robert Cain, Chairman, United Manufacturing

My friends,

You may have heard that we are facing some significant market challenges. The Board of Directors has made some personnel changes, effective immediately.

Our auditors have uncovered accounting irregularities in the way manufacturing cost savings from kaizen pilot cells were reported. Several million dollars of projected production savings were incorrectly subtracted from actual current product costs in United's income statement. The investigation into these accounting errors continues; United will revise the past fiscal year's income statement and shareholder updates.

As a result of the ongoing investigation, the Board of Directors has reassigned Siegfried Wolfe to Field Service Operations. Sieg's reassignment will become permanent after United's outsourcing plan is complete. Production of classic motors, as well as new products in development, will shift to our

---

South American and Asian partners, leaving aftermarket support here in the U. S.

Richard Bufflelunk has retired from United. We wish to thank him for his 28 years of dedicated service.

We extend our best wishes to Ms. Brendanne Soufflet, a promising young supply management star. Ms. Soufflet will be taking some time off before she starts grad school. We wish her continued success wherever she goes.

I am sure you all join with me in mourning the passing of a member of the United family, Ed Candyman. He will be sorely missed. We were shocked and saddened to hear of his premature demise. Ed was stricken in the Taipei airport on a supplier management trip to the Far East, where he and Ms. Soufflet endeavored to recapture purchasing costs from key United suppliers.

And finally, we want to welcome the new Central Strategic Sourcing Commodity Team headed by Sean Bittbeiter. This group has started to deliver millions of dollars of real, measurable cost savings. We are proud to have them playing a key role in the next generation of United Manufacturing. For the time being, the team reports directly to the office of the president, with oversight by our CFO. Strategic Sourcing will be expanding its work beyond its startup commodities—MRO, Transportation/ Logistics/ Packaging, plastics, telecom, electronics—into all areas of United's purchasing spend. All manufacturing—including outsourced product—as well as transportation, logistics and distribution, and all purchased goods, will be managed by Central Strategic Sourcing, including the outsourcing of US production to other areas.

Bittbeiter's team is also tasked with a complete IT assessment and capabilities review. We'll be updating you all on this critical project as soon as we have information to share.

Best regards to all,

Bob Crain
Chairman

Bittbeiter looked up and saw his team staring at him in stunned silence.

Parmenter was the first to speak up. "Wow. It's about time. You could see it coming."

"Poor Candyman. Heard they found him doubled over a sink in the men's room in some airport. Jeesh, what a way to go."

"What a way to be found, you mean—"

"Yeah, and what's this about purported—no, projected production savings in the income statement? Don't tell me they tried to extrapolate—hey, I get it—you know the kaizen improvements like floor space and throughput?"

"Sounds like they took the savings from the pilot cells and used them to project reduced manufacturing costs up into the income statement."

"What?" Kathy's eyes opened wider now.

"Yeah, it's in the numbers. They showed big, happy projected profits to the shareholders and analysts. Only the projected profits weren't real, 'cause they didn't make the numbers. And the component suppliers weren't really on board, so they didn't make the numbers, either."

"You mean the pilot cells worked, but they couldn't extend the lean results to the whole factory and the suppliers?"

Dave jumped in. "That's it. That's why they call it sustaining the gains.

"How are you gonna get a couple thousand suppliers to that level?"

"Ohhh, not good to mess with Wall Street—before they had even redesigned the lines for real? Whoa. They had to be desperate or stupid to think nobody would figure it out."

Dave zeroed in on the inconsistency. "Wait. Wasn't there a shareholder suit against a company that cooked the books and the shareholders found out? The income statements looked great because of manufacturing's reduced costs, and by the time the SEC figured it out, a couple execs had unloaded their stock at twice what they paid for it. Bufflelunk might have been selling off little bits quietly, just enough to be under the radar. Because he knew it was going to tank as soon as Wolfe's cost savings evaporated."

"Well, this gets Bufflelunk and Blondie out of the way," the manager declared. "Although I'm going to miss her expense-account dinners. That woman knew how to use a credit card! But now we can show them some real savings, some strategic sourcing, and I for one am looking forward to nailing some maverick buying!"

Dave and Ravi smiled. They knew that their commodities, plastics and MRO, would be key to United's new sourcing initiatives. "Listen, guys," Dave said, savoring the moment, "I think my people can free up some cash in MRO while you folks work through the more difficult areas. I figure the first year we'll pick the low-hanging fruit, but by year two, we'd better have the tougher areas in line."

Bittbeiter spoke up. "That's right, Dave. You've all done this drill before. The President and the CFO are giving us the okay to consolidate buys and leverage the spend. I've got some custom software being developed in Bangalore that will let us run what-ifs and dollarize the results, monitor risks, measure the tradeoffs. We should be ready to run the first analysis in two weeks—or less if the Indians come through like I think they will. It'll give us a better idea of which suppliers give us the best prices and quality and which ones are on the brink of going under. We're calling it 'total cost of ownership' for the new subcontractors. I think we can take some significant costs out of most of the products right away. There may be some rationalization later. Over the years we've developed a lot of variety. United will make anything for anybody, and that's expensive."

Annette stood and cleared her throat. Armed with graph paper, her eyes scanned the collage of numbers, resting on one meaningful percentage she knew the team would love, 20 percent. Around the war room, she was

known as "Miss Nervous" because she saw all the impos-
sibilities—too many. In fact, she got blinded by them and
bogged down too easily. But she knew the telecom business
inside out, and her ability to identify and cut through the
sales pitches had won her kudos in the CFO's office, where
money talked.

"But . . . you can't . . . Well, it's a good thing I started a
new RFP for cell phones. Looks like we're going to need it."

"That's right, Annette, we're going to need every nickel of it. I want to prepare a commodity team savings report
for the Board. So I'll need each of you to prepare a written
commodity plan and a savings summary of cost-cutting
ideas from the Blog."

"A written commodity plan—like, is there any other
kind?" Ravi piped up. The team understood Bittbeiter's
insistence on written, not verbal, commodity plans. If it
wasn't down on paper, it wasn't real and probably would-
n't withstand the push-back strategic buyers so frequently
experienced from the trenches.

"Right, your written commodity plan, with actual and
projected savings, your usual look into the future."
Bittbeiter's hands waved over an imaginary crystal ball.
"You know, technology trends, supplier shifts, whatever
strategic moves you think the Board should be aware of.
And I need it by Monday."

Bittbeiter knew each one of them would struggle to
compress their findings into a short commodity plan. He
knew experts like the late Gene Richter, IBM's turnaround
CPO, and Dave Nelson at Honda insisted on a written plan
for each commodity. The plan became an invaluable lever
when issues of central/decentral buying came up. It was
easier to squash maverick buying when the savings from
consolidating the buy into higher volumes with fewer suppliers were so clear.

One by one, the commodity plans with highlighted

savings summaries dropped into Bitbeiter's e-mail. The team was in motion, calculators in hand, sniffing out the money and reeling it in.

Bittbeiter scanned the plans, adding them up into "safe," "realistic" and "reach" categories of projected savings with three running totals. Without big-system software, the team had to rely on spreadsheets, but all that would soon change. More important, he thought, was the rationale behind each new and developing strategy, because that's where his commodity planners were becoming more knowledgeable than their suppliers themselves. With a combination of insight into technology and market shifts, along with day-to-day market price indices, Sean knew that current projections were framed by a big-picture perspective.

Slowly, the strategic sourcing report came together. He knew the numbers had to pass the Board's paranoia test. Bald-faced projections and hope were not enough. United needed real cost savings in the commodities that most directly affected the business. Most of them had to come from picking the right suppliers, some of whom they'd never even meet on purpose, a phrase he borrowed from Brad Holcomb, survivor of a similar big turnaround.

Gradually, commodity by commodity, the numbers materialized on laptop screens. First, MRO. Bittbeiter felt a solid starting commodity would be MRO—lots of low-hanging fruit—followed by communications and Transportation/Logistics, plastics, and electronics.

Before she skipped, Blondie had attempted to restructure some deals from the Far East, but there was no telling what the woman had actually come up with. "So let's keep it overly simple for the C-level guys," he thought. "Let's give them Ten Ways to Cut The Spend Ten percent Right Now," he said, as he moved the cursor and began to type:

Executive Summary
United's New Strategic Sourcing Strategy

United Manufacturing's procurement is being restructured to take advantage of better buying methods across all major commodities. The objective is to bring United's purchasing spend down by at least ten to 15 percent, with continued savings year to year as more commodities are rolled into the plan and as United acquires more good suppliers and better information about the buy.

United is adopting a 12-step sourcing process to control all the company's spend. This is a tremendous change for United, because the company will concentrate all purchasing research and buying for key commodities, including MRO, telecom, plastics, and electronic parts, Transportation/Logistics/Packaging and Benefits, with commodity managers, one for each category. They will research the spend and identify and contract with new sources. They will communicate with current suppliers and coordinate with Engineering and Marketing for requirements and trends one to three years out. Their short-term focus is consolidation and leveraging the volume of United's combined spending power for spend reduction. In the short term, they will start to build an information base that can be used later to fuel spend management software for quicker decision-making. THE COMMODITY MANAGERS ARE THE ONLY BUYERS AUTHORIZED TO PURCHASE AND APPROVE PAYMENTS FOR UNITED.

For all commodities, starting with MRO, telecom, plastics, electronic parts, Transportation/Packaging/Logistics and Benefits, and expanding to the remainder as the larger groups are put under central control, we have outlined a new 12-step sourcing process that will allow United to understand and control its purchasing spend. It will take three to six months to find all relevant spend data, and some of the information may be less current, but this is a reasonable starting point. Simply consolidating the spend for key commodities will free up significant amounts of cash.

United's New 12-Step Strategic Sourcing Process:

1. Analyze the spend

Determine the spend by commodity and in total—what we buy, from whom, in what quantities, at what prices and when. This information is only partially available, but Accounts Payable invoices and shipping receipts, as well as original contracts and closed orders, will provide most of the information needed to reach an approximate total of United's combined spend for key commodities.

2. Establish cost reduction target

This year, United's CEO set a Year One 15 percent cost reduction target. The year-to-year target should drop into the single digits, depending on gains achieved for Year One.

3. Audit

The prices and quantities agreed to in contracts, particularly older ones, may not be the ones appearing in invoices and payments. A sampling of all receipts and payments to compare against contracts will highlight discrepancies and immediate savings opportunities.

4. Supplier Selection

United's supply base numbers over 30,000 suppliers, many of which are used infrequently. The commodity team will review current supplier performance—quality, delivery, pricing, and engineering support—sort the supply base into suppliers to retain, suppliers to cut, and suppliers for whom the company needs more time or data for a decision. For items outsourced or contracted to a third-party provider, these suppliers will drop off United's supply base. The commodity team needs supplier performance history relative to price, quality, on-time delivery and subjective partnering/alignment criteria. Key questions during the selection process are: Are they suppliers we want to continue with? Are their prices competitive with other suppliers? Do they offer potential for growth with us? For each major commodity, United will buy from no more than three to six suppliers;

5. Supplier Survey

United's sourcing team needs to understand if the company is giving suppliers what they need—information, technical assists, forecasts—to do the best job for the customer. The supplier survey, conducted at least once a year by a third party, asks suppliers to evaluate United as a key partnering customer relative to communications, pricing requirements, etc. See *Breakthrough Partnering*, Patricia E. Moody, John Wiley and Sons/omneo, 1993, for Motorola, GM/Williams and Solectron supplier surveys.

6. Site visits

As the sourcing team narrows United's supply base to a smaller group of high-performing supplier/partners, commodity managers will contact suppliers or consortia/outsourcing specialists and begin consolidated volume discussions based on United's commodity plan and its ongoing requirements for pricing, technology and scheduling. For commodities representing significant price or quality risk to United, commodity managers will visit suppliers at least once a year. Each new supplier agreement will be preceded by a site visit. For example, because some of Dave's plastic parts are highly engineered for United's specifications, Dave and an engineer will visit supplier candidates, review engineering requirements and evaluate that supplier's technology and capacity capabilities.

7. Leverage the spend

We are consolidating along two paths: (a) by reducing United's supply base from 30,000 to less than 1,500 and (b) by reducing the number of buyers inside United who can purchase material to one expert buyer, a commodity manager, per commodity group. United will centralize and consolidate all buying and in-house manufacturing. United has decided to outsource most manufacturing, which increases purchasing responsibilities as commodity managers source and place United's basic assembly work with subcontract manufacturers. Manufacturing will report to the CFO or the new CPO.

Commodity managers will complete a written commodity strategy for each commodity, to include future outlook. Commodity managers in the team who reach savings goals will be eligible for a bonus savings pool; teams that beat market prices will also be eligible for a new market price savings pool. There is a three-to-one return on the investment in central commodity managers; first year savings from MRO will cover the initial outlay.

Centralizing the buy may be United's most difficult change, but it is essential for nearly every commodity, from Manufacturing components to pencils and scratch pads. United Manufacturing has been operating with a very decentralized approach to buying. Every division, every product line and market segment, every production line and shipping area, has been buying its own favorite materials. In some areas there are signature limits on what a requisitioner can spend—$5,000 and under—but not even that general rule was steadfastly followed. And, of course, this explains how United accumulated over 30,000—and counting—suppliers from all over the world; everyone has his favorites.

Engineering, for instance, likes to buy plastic parts from Acme Speed Molding, because Acme can deliver small quantities quickly for a premium. Production, however, buys huge volumes of plastic components from a dozen generally cheaper, global suppliers. Field Service buys aftermarket parts from yet another supplier to support its service requirements. And some buyers have special relationships with local sources whom they feel a need to protect.

Other requirements data need to be collected and confirmed—Field Service, for instance—and this will take six to eight months to roll into overall requirements.

All of United's unconsolidated buying has quietly accumulated higher costs. The best way to consolidate a scattered spend is to limit all buying to a central buying group using a single data base, reporting in to the Chief Procurement Officer, under the CFO. This is how Gene Richter structured the procurement operation during IBM's turnaround. Working under CFO Jerry York, Richter saved IBM $12B. No checks will be cut for payments without commodity manager approval; this policy is supported and monitored by United's CFO.

For commodities with no data in the purchasing central data base, United will hire two summer interns who will dig data from the Accounts Payable files (or suppliers if necessary), to establish prices and quantities, suppliers, etc. As an interim step, the information will be collected on Excel spreadsheets; spreadsheets will be replaced or supplemented by spend management on-demand software (cost under $50K).

United will consolidate its spend commodity by commodity, starting with MRO, telecom, plastic injection molded parts, electronics, Transportation/Logistics/Packaging/Distribution and Benefits. These groups should represent about 60 percent of United's total purchased spend. We will expand the number of commodities to cover 80 percent or more.

For example, all plastic injection molded parts will be planned and bought by Dave, United's strategic sourcing plastics commodity manager. No other purchases will be approved or paid for if they are made outside Dave's commodity plan. All requirements for these parts will be reflected in the planning system, including Field Service quantities and engineering prototypes.

8. Place the business

There are three ways United will place its commodity spend—through the normal RFP and Request for Quotes process, by outsourcing the spend to a third-party provider, such as subcontract manufacturing, or by an internet auction. Some commodities, such as cleaning materials, can be sourced through a one-time internet auction. Depending on the results of the commodity research, United may contract all MRO office supplies with an on-line distributor that meets our savings goal and offers an on-line catalog.

The second buying process United will use for certain commodities, such as travel, telecom and health insurance, is to engage an outside consultant to set up the review, define needs and help with provider selection. Projected savings from working with an outside expert will cover startup costs and cut three to six months from the startup time. We want to use this help to free up immediate savings in these areas while we dig into data to find more difficult savings in engineered and other production parts.

The first-month return will cover the initial setup

investment, and the plan is to ask the consultant to perform a yearly "health check" contract and supplier review for these commodities.

9. Contracts

United's current procurement arrangements include an assortment of verbal and written contracts, some as many as 24 pages long. The only way United can maintain the kind of spend management information that will meet ten to 15 percent savings goals and establish baseline data points is by consolidating all buying deals into a United-approved contract format. Strategic Sourcing and Legal have developed a revised United standard contract, an on-line, three-page document that we will review with all new and old key suppliers.

10. Verify, track and control

Audit the savings process; verify cost savings, track real-location of savings (reduce budgets), and continue to monitor purchasing activity on new agreements. For example, if Sourcing secures $50K savings on travel expenses, the travel budget should be reduced by $50K to maintain the gain. If the $50K savings simply move from the travel budget to another line item, the savings will be lost, and Commodity Management will not be able to maintain ongoing savings in that category. It is the responsibility of the commodity manager to confirm that negotiated savings appear on actual payment transactions. On shared savings from the suggestion system, or possible supplier development improvements, the CFO requires verification of savings.

11. Commodity Plan

Each commodity under control of Strategic Sourcing will be documented with key supplier and market information in the written commodity plan. The commodity plan basics include metrics on current suppliers, ongoing requirements and site visit notes.

United will track performance metrics for current suppliers—total dollars spent, quality and on-time deliveries, pricing issues, current and future requirements, future technology trends, cost breakdown models where available or standard cost data or negotiated prices

Initially, not all this information will be easily obtained, because so much of United's spend has been managed "off-line." Where system data are missing, Accounts Payable or Receiving files will furnish reasonable starting information on actual buys.

United will not always award business to lowest-cost providers. For some products, United will be looking for technology leadership from suppliers, not simply lowest price. The commodity plan will identify key technology needs and align them with supplier selection strategies.

For plastic injection molded parts, for instance, Dave will prepare a requirements summary extending out through the next two years. The requirements summary gives suppliers an idea of gross quantities and items needed, without attempting to define all the specific forecasting flavors beyond lead times. Essentially, it is a capacity reservation for the supplier. Next, Dave will review current contracts and pricing, and, based on market index projections, he will consolidate and put the business out to bid. Other commodity managers, depending on their commodities, may use an outsourcing provider/consortium or an internet auction to identify and contract with good suppliers.

Dave and his Engineering counterpart will be available to answer supplier questions. We expect to receive quotes within four to six weeks of most RFQs. Dave will review any unanswered questions and make a recommendation for his primary and secondary supplier sources, in conjunction with Engineering input.

12. Set new cost reduction goals, and review new supplier performance data

This is an iterative process that requires annual review. Expand to new commodity areas. Initial savings from simply paying closer attention to buying patterns and working with good suppliers will get United ten to 15 percent savings. Sustaining the savings year after year and rolling new commodities into the plan will take United Strategic Sourcing into the next level of maturity. To reach excellent or expert buying levels, United should be able to project and consistently achieve three, or five-percent-plus savings year to year. We believe that for United, moving from its beginner's level to expert operations will require good information, good people and better systems, including on-demand spend management software, as well as some optimization planning for Transportation and Logistics.

SAVINGS OPPORTUNITIES

United's preliminary spend analysis shows overall opportunity for cost savings in the six to ten percent or higher range. Next month's first on-line auction for one commodity will yield a one-time higher savings percentage, but at this point we're staying with our conservative projections.

Overall, Strategic Sourcing will bring continued cost reductions for the next three to five years. As United expands its outsourcing efforts, savings will stabilize at a comfortable three to five percent per year.

The first year of United's new sourcing process will be

a year of consolidation and trimming the supply base. Initial savings from consolidation of the spend and outsourcing manufacturing will meet United's ten to 15 percent savings objectives. In some commodity areas, initial savings will reach the 25 to 30 percent range. Ongoing annual savings and better data, working with fewer and better suppliers, will let United maintain steady spending reductions.

Initially, Strategic Sourcing will focus on finding and putting basic agreements in place with the right suppliers. Commodity managers will negotiate and contract with key suppliers, initially for all production quantities. Other requirements data will need to be collected and confirmed—Field Service, for instance—and this will take six to eight months to roll into overall requirements

United Manufacturing's supply base will be consolidated to under 1,500 supplier partners by the end of next year and fewer than 1,000 six months after that. Strategic partner contracts will be awarded on competitive pricing and other decision factors, such as performance as captured in the scorecard; better performance awards best partners bigger shares of United's business.

Recommendations

The team's sourcing plan contains spend analysis opportunities in the areas of MRO, telecom, outsourced manufacturing, Transportation and Logistics, plastics and possibly healthcare benefits. Other commodities are being reviewed for possible inclusion in the sourcing plan. United's outsourced manufacturing project will move Manufacturing to new external suppliers; as these products are transferred out, they will come under the control of Strategic Sourcing.

United is following the Richter model of supply management maturity. United's sourcing activities have matured from traditional transaction-based purchasing to competent team-based spend management capable of achieving predictable savings in the three to five percent range. The team achieved these gains with a mix of manual and spreadsheet tools; in the next phase, we will supplement good buying with spend management, optimization, network design and analysis software. We will have nearly eliminated maverick buying and outsourced much of Manufacturing. Our continued focus on key commodities will yield sustained gains.

Savings ideas continue to arrive via the Blog. We've widened our access to other companies' expertise and experience by benchmarking through the Blog. The commodity teams will continue to benchmark other top procurement operations and focus on the quickest opportunities for cost savings. MRO continues to be an area that we want to get out of the way as we work on more difficult commodities.

The United Manufacturing Strategic Sourcing Blog is an incredible source of ideas and inspiration, with some spam. The team regularly posts questions and culls answers. During the first month, over 2,000 responses flooded the system; since then, we've begun correspondence with a few high-quality "regulars."

The Blog identifies new approaches to managing key commodities. Some of these concepts can be adopted immediately, and some will require more work. United's startup strategy is to implement the easy savings ideas first, which buys time to work on the more difficult areas. Although the Blog is a great way to reach out to a wider audience, it takes time to select and compress (and also filter the spammers). The content in the Blog is raw and unedited. Stay tuned.

TEN SAVINGS AREAS:

These are the savings ideas that the commodity managers are using to realize first-year savings. Most of these ideas are contained in the blogs. A few are from supplier visits.

1. Consolidate the spend - Centralize and consolidate all buying and in-house manufacturing.

Do a written commodity strategy for each commodity, to include future outlook. Outlaw maverick buying. Reward buyers who beat the market. Award bonus compensation to commodity teams that beat market prices. Consider a buying consortium.

Consolidating the spend is the first and biggest savings idea that can apply to every commodity. Although it may be difficult initially to find all key commodity information, the Strategic Sourcing commodity plans will accumulate enough of the numbers to thin the supply base and leverage the spend. For some commodities, United will outsource or use a third-party provider that can consolidate spend on its behalf. Some experts say that consolidation in a decentralized operation will earn 20 to 30 percent reductions to start.

The biggest and easiest areas to start with are MRO and Transportation/Logistics and packaging. The gains from these areas will pay back the investment cost for the commodity managers and carry over as they work more challenging commodities.

Manage "A" parts (those few items representing 80 percent of the cost) daily; hold one week or less inventory.

Review lead times and adjust for schedules. Do not bring in material early.

Dollar Days! – prioritize and clear up past dues, and generate cash by calculating the true value of past due orders (number of days past due x dollars past due).

Join or establish a consortium for some items, starting with office supplies.

Raw material costs – steel, fuel, aluminum, resins. Consolidate and negotiate on behalf of suppliers. Give suppliers the option of buying off your contract, at your negotiated prices.

Standardize along fewer varieties, especially for steel grades, batteries, plastic resins.

Reverse-auction commodity items.

Negotiate consignment purchase agreements in which the customer pays only when parts are used; storage is negotiable

For a small or medium-sized business/spend, participate in your larger partner's auction.

2. MRO and other soft expenses, such as travel, legal, public relations, telecom

The quickest route to savings for United's MRO spend is a combination of consolidating and rebidding soft spend commodities, starting with travel and telecom, printing and public relations. Legal will require closer review.

For indirect spend associated with Manufacturing and Engineering, the commodity plan will use an on-line distributor with authorized users accessing United's custom-designed web catalog.

For consolidation and upgrading of telecom and benefits, United will engage an outside consultant to set up and review annual contract spending. Payback for the consultant cost is six months or less, not including cash realized with disposition of outdated and excess equipment.

> Go paperless in procurement! Replace paper with electronic transactions for orders and receiving documents!
>
> Use P-cards (purchasing credit cards) to eliminate transaction costs for invoicing and check writing.
>
> Ask suppliers to develop an "approved item" on-line catalog for your business.
>
> Lightbulbs – negotiate globally, ship locally. Replace all when one fails.

Travel:

Consolidation of travel expenses should easily generate Year One savings for airplane tickets, reservation costs, and hotel and car rental costs. Strategic Sourcing has negotiated, based on review of one year's consolidated spend data, reduced prices from major carriers and hotels. Based on these agreements, Strategic Sourcing has placed these suppliers on United's list of approved vendors. When United employees book travel on their own or through United's provider, they must use the approved carriers to receive United's new negotiated prices, and for their expense reimbursements to be processed. No exceptions! Commodity management will review travel expenses against summary reports for additional opportunities and for VTC.

Legal and public relations:

United is in the process of consolidating all legal and public relations business, including marketing brochures, annual reports, contract reviews, etc., with two approved suppliers. In the area of public relations, United wants to consolidate web content and design with a single firm that can provide editorial content and design for its printed materials.

Telecom:

Telecom is a huge savings opportunity area from the consolidation perspective, as well as negotiation of better price plans for high volumes. United employees and sub-contractors use a variety of technologies and telecommunications tools, from cell phones and land lines to computers, PDAs, web services, software applications, and installation, maintenance and repair services. Sourcing has decided to use an outside consultant to review and put out for bid all phone—landline, cell and fax— business; this technology will be consolidated with one provider for national services. We will negotiate a separate contract for international telecom. Once the outside consultant has set up the telecom agreement and contract, he will provide United with semiannual equipment and pricing updates so that our own commodity managers can keep up with product upgrades and planned price cuts.

Cell phone pooling—negotiate a total minutes used cost from providers to avoid excess use charges.

Compare web-collaboration tools to big phone company teleconferencing charges.

Term commitments earn reduced rates.

Phone cards—use cell phones or phone cards for hotel room phone calls.

Computers and software:

United has the same proliferation problem with computers and some software purchases that it has in the area of telecom. We think Strategic Sourcing can consolidate and execute a sensible plan for IT equipment directly with suppliers, such as Dell and IBM, that will generate big savings for laptops and desktop equipment, possibly servers and other gear. Once we have that contract in place, we will phase out old equipment and cover all equipment purchases under the new, approved contract. Initial purchase prices, as well as maintenance and user costs, will drop.

Following up on a blog recommendation and reviewing a sampling of software package purchases, we discovered that we've acquired the same application from several different sources at significantly different prices. Consolidating the spend for all software purchases should eliminate this kind of discrepancy.

Software to evaluate costs based on CAD drawings. CostPoint from Akoya is one package that takes data from a CAD file and runs it through a number of algorithms to identify possible cost savings, a useful approach prior to making some outsourcing decisions.

Copiers, faxes and mail machines—Consolidate spend, consider using outside consultant to prepare RFP and set up new agreements.

Printing costs—Consolidate print runs to reduce setup costs.

Lease vs. buy analysis for equipment.

Training—Seek government grants for training, especially for small and medium-sized businesses working on productivity improvements.

Insurance—If a supplier can be covered under the customer's indemnity policy, both parties can save money on insurance premiums and avoid potential lawsuits.

Health insurance and wellness programs—Institute a wellness program that incents employees for good diet and exercise habits. Offer voluntary health risk assessments and prevention advice based on insurer's negotiated cost reductions. Self-insure; self-funded health plans save money.

Annual cleanup day —Throw out, sell or trade what you really don't need. Sell it on eBay.

Recycle and sell trash—paper, plastic, metals, cardboard—to eliminate disposal fees and recapture cash.

3. Outsource

Gains projected from manufacturing's kaizen improvement teams were slow in coming, and they were not extended throughout United's vast network of suppliers. United's profit crisis requires quicker cost reduction measures. Its decision to outsource the majority of its manufacturing processes will realize significant gains. Kaizen or lean manufacturing projects can be used to clarify a production or office process, but for immediate and significant savings of the magnitude that United needs, kaizen is not the sole contributor. Even after consolidation of United's supply base to a manageable number of suppliers, kaizen approaches can be selectively applied. Outsourcing these processes requires good information and better decision-making for Logistics and Transportation because of the potential for increased freight charges. The Strategic Sourcing transportation and logistics commodity plan includes a phase-in for these subcontracted products.

United is reviewing other outsourcing options, including procurement of Indirect materials and IT.

> Outsource manufacturing—Negotiate to buy components from contract manufacturers, and direct their replenishment. Start a trading center like Motorola's in Singapore. Leverage and consolidate the buy and transfer components for subcontractors.

United is exploring outsourced manufacturing in China as well as Eastern Europe. In conjunction with total cost reviews for product to be sourced there, Strategic Sourcing is comparing additional logistics and transportation costs. For electronic components bought in volume in the Far East to supply offshore assembly, United would like to partner in a trading center like the ones that HP, IBM, and Motorola established in Singapore. The objective is to take back negotiated volume buys for subcontracted materials, to keep the margins.

Outsource other non-core activities—IT, indirect purchasing, logistics, security, payroll, even janitorial services.

Outsource procurement!

4. Transportation/Logistics/Distribution/Packaging

There are three completely unexplored areas in this commodity where United can realize savings—trucking and air freight, packaging and warehousing. We estimate that United's freight costs can be immediately reduced by 20 percent. To do this, United will consolidate its inbound and outbound shipping with a few key national and international providers that can offer expertise in designing networks and the on-line tracking that United needs.

United's packaging costs are ripe for reduction, starting with cardboard and corrugated. Our logistics and packaging commodity manager will review packaging requirements with Engineering and our main corrugated supplier to check specifications and costs. For those manufacturing areas remaining at United sites, returnable plastic totes from suppliers will replace cardboard. This will cut purchased and disposal costs and provide better protection for parts in transit.

We are also looking into consolidating with another producer for shipments coming from the Southeast. Our trucker is helping us work through a more cost-efficient load distribution and schedule.

Premium rates! A quick analysis of the number of United and supplier emergency air shipments showed that we could drop down one category of freight rates and save money. We are working with our shipping coordinator and the mail room to clarify when premium delivery is required, but we think we can save 10 to 15 percent here by making a few changes. Be sure that air freight is not listed as the standard shipping method.

Ask for tracking service on non-air freight shipments, starting with small parcels.

Shipping costs—Audit shipping bills to be sure shippers are charging the correct rate.

Labor costs in the warehouse—Set up small staging areas for fast-moving traffic. Put bulky items to be moved by lift trucks closest to dock. Set up a forward pick zone to cut labor costs—put the fastest movers in a concentrated area to reduce distance.

Use the right, well-maintained equipment for your warehousing needs. Consider double-pallet jacks and carousels and simple conveyor systems for material movement.

Use your warehouse space better—with lift trucks, maximum height utilization, different storage modules for different products and optimized pallet solutions.

Packaging—Take a hard look at the thickness and cost of packaging materials, such as plastic film, for product packaging as well as shipping and pallets. These items tend to be overspecified, generating as much as 40 percent extra costs.

Line-side deliveries of certified materials save labor and quality costs.

Eliminate wooden pallets and nonreturnable containers.

Consolidate shipments from one plant or division to another to reduce freight costs.

Keep the driver moving! Consider a drop-trailer program to eliminate turnaround times; tune up warehousing to speed processing and turnaround times.

Schedule milk runs for smaller quantities; negotiate freight rates in exchange for good schedule.

Do a cost segmentation analysis for rail vs. over-the-road shipping. Stratify the transportation spend to limit premium shipments to ten percent or less; try to shift more product to cheaper rail options.

Inbound freight—work with suppliers to schedule inbound shipments on cheaper modes. Customers with good outbound shipping agreements may extend them with certain shippers for inbound freight as well.

Avoid live-loading charges by scheduling a dropped trailer for every ten filled shipments, or some other economical and flexible arrangement.

Access optimization software on an on-demand or subscription basis, to model network and pallet/truck loading, packing alternatives.

Track warehouse order cycle times—how long it takes for an order to process through a distribution center; look at velocity through the pipeline as well as demand planning to control flows.

Work with box suppliers to optimize packaging strength relative to reduced costs.

Packaging engineers must participate in design teams to influence cost and design of shipping containers and packaging materials.

UPS and other providers offer design engineering services in product laboratories to customers concerned with costs as well as quality. Start with products that have heavy damage incidence, and work on design solutions.

5. Product Design—Design cost out of products with early supplier involvement, etc.

Ninety percent of product costs, including shipping and packing, are set during a product's early design phase. United's commodity management team will work with suppliers, product designers and manufacturing engineers to reduce product costs. The commodity plans will also reduce and eliminate complexity in key cost areas such as metals and plastic, batteries and fasteners. The benchmarks the sourcing team is using for early design involvement in procurement are Honda's 1998 Accord and the Toyota Camry, in which purchasing/design teams reduced total vehicle cost by over 25 percent.

> Reduce and eliminate complexity. Use life cycle management to eliminate obsolescence
> Buy a competitor's product, display it for a week on the floor, and conduct a cost and engineering tear-down. Share results with employees.
> Invoice and follow up for samples.

6. Costing

Develop real, in-depth, true cost expertise, including what Japanese cost experts call "should cost". Honda calls it target cost, and Toyota cost standards or cost models. True costs or cost standards are not the negotiated or con-tracted (market) costs, but they cover detailed breakdowns of all material and labor and actual processing costs broken down into all subcategories. Cost experts believe these costs are important to capture accurately at the beginning of a sourcing process, because they establish a baseline for improving product costs as materials and processes are reviewed. The approach is particularly relevant in heavy manufacturing applications.

The Cost models that United commodity managers are developing will include cost breakdowns and all trans-portation/logistics and packaging costs—total costs—which represent big savings opportunities for some com-modities. Working from industry and supplier data, along with past invoices and contracts, it takes a commodity manager approximately one week to develop a cost model;

projected savings range from five to 20 percent.

Diagram the supplier network involved in a product,

On castings, review costs for weight and prices.

For PC boards, review configuration and costs relative to size (cost per square inch).

On volume buys, group like components —all capacitors, for instance—for same price, rather than prices for different specs.

On parts that are run through another process, pay the sub-tier directly, to eliminate markups.

Use Cost Breakdown Worksheets to take costs out of assembled products.

and look carefully at second and third-tier suppliers to see if their contributions could be handled by the next tier up—consolidate!

Benchmark through professional associations to review pricing opportunities.

7. Supplier management, including supplier development, supplier-managed inventory.

The biggest savings opportunities in the supply base include lean improvement initiatives that cut waste and savings generated by leveraging better volumes. Initial savings from lean efforts can be impressive, but it is difficult to sustain the gains with some suppliers, and it takes a long time to extend lean practices across an entire supply base, as Sieg and his team discovered, especially if production is global. United's commodity managers will use a supplier report card to track key performance measures and identify developing problems. These reports will be supplemented by onsite visits and, for some commodities, in-plant supplier representatives.

Supplier suggestion systems and supplier training are

two approaches that United can use with its trimmed-down supply base. The projected payoff for the investment in training is three to one. Supplier suggestion systems take minimal original startup costs and generate the same or higher payoffs; suggestion systems are a "must-have" with United's big supply base. The system will be adopted internally as well.

> Supplier report card, including on-time delivery, quality. Don't pay top dollar for bad, late, early material, or material not packaged properly.

Use in-plants or supplier reps to work in-house on design and production issues, cut communication costs. They are on suppliers' payroll, but they carry a United badge and have access to United systems and personnel.

8. VTC, Verify, Track and Control

All cost savings must be certified by the CFO, and they must be checked against contract, invoice and actual payment data. Track cost reductions against budget to preserve savings. Unverified savings evaporate easily, and on key commodities, VTC is a requirement for good data as well as sustaining the gains.

For more examples of this disciplined approach, see *The Incredible Payback,* Nelson, Moody and Stegner, Amacom, 2004.

9. Accelerate quote to cash, review payment terms

Dell's build-to-order and cash realization models are great examples of optimizing cash flows. United's CFO will review all contract payment terms, looking for discounts for early payment and other advantageous arrangements with customers and suppliers. Aging the receivables will uncover other savings opportunities.

On payment terms and cash conversion cycles, United's CFO has authorized a review of United's payment arrangements and its quote-to-cash conversion times. There are several opportunities here to capture cash quicker and to eliminate late payment penalties and interest rate costs.

Can you get paid electronically before the product has been built? Before it ships? Yes!

Review and reduce inventory, receivables and payables; calculate number of days in each. Reduce inventory by supplier-managed inventory; reduce receivables by changing payment terms, discount for quicker payment. Suppliers will grant 2-4 % discounts for payments in less than 30 days.

Accounts payable reports to Procurement.

---

10. Suggestion System for suppliers and internal employees.

For many companies, the first positive step toward cost improvements is a suggestion system for suppliers and internal employees. It's a cheap way to let the real experts look at work processes and waste. Suggestion systems can now be hosted on the web for a commodity manager or team to review monthly. The initial investment is two days or less per month of their time, plus rewards for winning suggestions. Most major transplants and their key suppliers use suggestion systems to jump-start their improvement efforts because of the psychological impact these positive efforts have with the workforce, and because they free up creativity for long-term changes.

> Give suppliers incentives for good Value Engineering, Value Analysis suggestions.
> For internal employees, run a suggestion system that recognizes and rewards good suggestions with creative compensation solutions, such as tickets to events, dinner, etc.

The biggest savings opportunities for United require leveraging the spend by consolidating its buy. If United tackles no other savings ideas, it could achieve solid savings in the intermediate three to five percent level. By adopting the 12-step strategic sourcing process, with a central commodity management team structure that will develop in-depth expertise on costs, pricing, and supplier capabilities, United will achieve greater and more predictable savings that can be sustained year to year.

MRO, including telecom, and office supplies and equipment, is a great starting point that can fund other more difficult commodity areas. One functional area remains relatively unexplored by traditional manufacturing operations. Transportation/Logistics/Packaging, and the savings that United will achieve by addressing this opportunity, should carry it toward the next level of supply management maturity.

Finally, for United to achieve expert levels, technology tools must be in place to eliminate manual research; the company needs tracking software tools to handle spend analysis, cost analysis, optimization of networks, e-procurement and risk management. They will move United's sourcing process into levels of performance achieved by only the top one to two percent of all corporations.

Epilogue

You ain't gonna teach the Chinese to be lean.
Patricia E. Moody

A very small number of companies have succeeded in reaching the excellent or expert level of supply management depicted in the graph on page 136.

So where does that leave most companies that simply want to reduce their spend? They may not have a central sourcing group or access to complete purchasing data on one single powerful system. Or they may not have resources to hire a team of supplier development engineers. Is there hope for them?

Any company can take at least one to two percent out of its purchasing spend initially just by buying smarter. By moving to centralized buying staffed by commodity experts using basic systems, expect to realize more savings. To move into the excellent category, the strategic sourcing team will need great systems and sound data, as well as the power to consolidate all sourcing, including that of any manufacturing, into one group. These high performers need to be compensated for great buying. For sustained gains, the expert strategic sourcing group will have all the tools, the consolidated information and consolidated buy, as well as political and organizational clout, at the boardroom level.

There are a few more key areas that have generally been ignored in the drive to reduce costs—transportation/logistics/distribution, packaging and health care benefits. It is clear that companies are not paying enough attention to packaging, and to deliberate network design, transportation and logistics. Because of the millions of dollars of materials that are outsourced to China and other distant areas, the entire area of packing and shipping must be considered part of the total cost equation. The Council of Supply Chain Management Professionals, formerly the Council of Logistics Management, headed by Maria McIntyre, is an incredible source of expertise for this new challenge.

Local product for local markets

There's one more strategic advantage that global organizations need to address, and that is the customer. We call it extreme customer management. There are still some strong opportunities open in the customer relationship area. Think about what happens to customer information—preferences, input toward next-generation design, even computerized customer profiles—when products are outsourced to low-cost countries. That invaluable customer information may be lost because the outsourcing decision was based on material and labor costs only. Or the information may never make it back to procurement and design teams. But it is a key competitive advantage for companies looking to maintain localized product control. When procurement works with design, products are cheaper and higher quality. When procurement and design work with customers, they unleash new power to absolutely anticipate and match what customers don't even think they want! It's the 1950s marketing paradigm rocketed 50 years ahead. It's also the answer to how Western organizations with inherently high labor costs driven by higher standards of living can preserve and grow their own local markets—by knowing their customers even better than the customers themselves, and certainly better than third-world factories and call centers can. For now we're calling this customer closeness, or LOCK-ON™. It's a data-rich but creatively driven approach, totally open to invaluable feed-

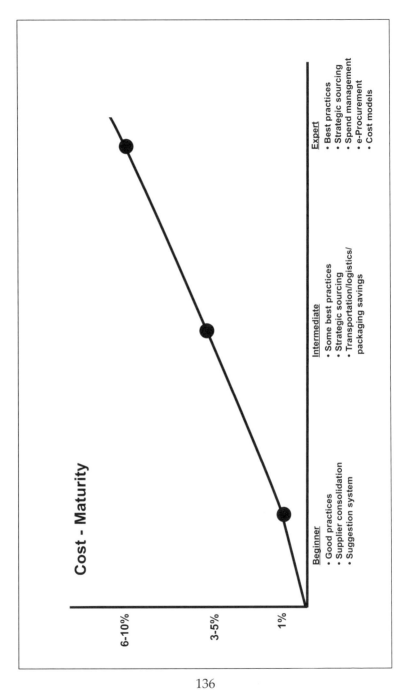

Cost - Maturity

6-10%

3-5%

1%

Beginner
• Good practices
• Supplier consolidation
• Suggestion system

Intermediate
• Some best practices
• Strategic sourcing
• Transportation/logistics/
  packaging savings

Expert
• Best practices
• Strategic sourcing
• Spend management
• e-Procurement
• Cost models

back from all sources—blogs, surveys, dreams.

When United Manufacturing sent Brendanne Soufflet and Ed Candyman out to renegotiate supplier contracts, they were taking the first step toward bringing down their costs, but without consolidating first. It was an easy mistake, and one that obscured United's basic issue—building a strong supply base that delivered quality as well as great pricing. Blondie and Ed's negotiations may have been more in the Lopez style of hammering suppliers into submission. We'll never know, since both parties made good their escape from a deteriorating crisis.

United's next step, a single-minded emphasis on shop-floor cost cutting, was equally narrow, especially for companies that have outsourced and reduced labor costs to less than ten or 20 percent of total costs. It's not the biggest opportunity area, but because it's here and visible, it's easy to focus on. And, of course, training the entire workforce before setting up a balanced approach to cost reduction is another common mistake that produces temporarily comforting results.

So what's a company to do? Take a balanced approach. Focus on the big numbers. Put a few very bright buyers in position to go after commodity groups. Give them the right numbers, and they will find a way.

The Big Squeeze Quiz

Each question counts for 14.3 points. Question 8 is a bonus question. Take as long as you want to answer each question. The scores will be absolute, not graded on a curve, kind of like life. We know that some of you will cheat. That's like life, too. To help you out, the answers appear upside down at the end of the quiz.

Your score:

1 correct - 14.3 – We have a spot in Kaizen Master Spirit classes on permanent hold for you, the seventh ring of Hell.

2 correct - 28.6 – You didn't cheat hard enough.

3 correct - 42.9 – I'm going down to the Teacher's Lounge for a cigarette. Please recheck your answers.

4 correct - 57.1 – You're in range. I'm going to assign summer reading to get you into Big Squeeze heaven.

5 correct - 71.4 – Your mother would be so proud!

6 correct - 85.71 - You're eligible for the honor roll.

7 correct - 99.999998 – Everybody hates a smartass. You can leave now.

8 correct - 109.9 - I see a familiar pattern here. Did you by any chance grow up in The Point?

* * *

1. What garlicky appetizer did Ms. Soufflet down before her main course, Richard Bufflelunk?

2. What companies established a trading center in Singapore to take back the bill of material from contract manufacturers and to mask true prices negotiated by centralized buying, thereby cutting subcontracted procurement margins?

3. What's a "signing bonus"?
a.) What Pedro Martinez needed to join the Mets;
b.) Paris Hilton's engagement ring; or
c.) An enticement some suppliers use to attract possible customers?

138

4. What is a Commodity Council?

a.) Gene Richter's organizational approach to managing hundreds of buyers without having all of them report in directly to him;

b.) A nonprofit fanatical national bicycling group established in North America to set fuel prices and lobby for import tariffs;

c.) A nonprofit fanatical international group established in Saudi Arabia to set fuel prices;

d.) an exclusive buyer's club?

5. What improper accounting practices ended Sieg's manufacturing career?

6. What is Total Cost of Ownership? Standard Cost? Cost Standards? Target Costs? Activity-Based Costing? Should Cost?

7. How many times can you say l-e-a-n while hopping on one foot, rubbing your left ear and singing the Rolling Stones' "You can't always get what you want"?

Ten-point Bonus question:
8. What is a heijunka box, and how is it used?

---

1. Answer: escargots

2. Answer: IBM, HP and Motorola

3. Answer: c

4. Answer: a

5. Answer: Projecting lean kaizen results to enterprise-wide supplier performance and reflecting the projected cost savings in the corporate income statement.

6. Answer: Confusing, isn't it? Total Cost of Ownership: Japanese approach that includes all costs—labor, materials, logistics, packaging, handling, etc. Standard Cost: A traditional Cost Accounting measurement. Cost Standards: A Japanese approach that develops costs in detail, describing actual costs for materials, labor, etc. Next step is to source components to suppliers with these cost standards in mind to take market share. Target Costs: Honda's version of Cost Standards. Activity-Based Costing: Reality-based attempt by Robin Cooper, et al., to extract real costs from Cost Accounting operations and convey them in a meaningful way that clarifies decisions.

7. Zero, unless you can say l-e-a-n and sing at the same time.

8. Answer: A heijunka box is origami disguised as a production schedule, used to track and plan manufacturing activities. Some companies use the heijunka box as a paperweight, while others in Northern climes use it for kindling. Still others use it to mimic Toyota Production System schedules, but everybody knows that even Toyota uses computers nowadays.

Blog Summary, Basic

Organization structure in procurement—we can't centralize, but we figured out that we could leverage our spend on certain commodities by getting good data consolidated on the computer. Nobody can argue with the numbers, and the computer allows us to see the totals even if we know that some divisions want to continue to buy on their own.

* * *

Mike Gray, C.P.M., CIRM
Supply Chain Evangelist – Dell, Inc.
Mike_Gray@Dell.com

It's about cash. That's why you do supply chain. As a supply chain practitioner, you are viewed as a money drain from the top of your business—after all, you spend money on stuff (Many companies spend around 50% of their top-line revenue with suppliers.) and lose it (Never had a cycle count adjustment?) or throw it away (Ever had a time when you didn't have any excess \ obsolete inventory?).

Face it, we (supply chain practitioners) are (or could be) viewed in a different light than our sales colleagues. Why? Because they (our sales friends) make money and we (SCM practitioners) spend money...who would you favor?

Now, if you were to change your viewpoint to how you can conserve cash, you might get more positive attention...Okay, I can hear you saying, but what about the savings we drive for purchase prices? All right, what about it? Do you think the top of your business really believes the savings numbers you put up? After all, they are mostly avoidance measures, aren't they? Can you absolutely prove you saved the amount of money you are posting? Have you ever tried to claim savings that were going to happen anyway? Anyone who projects savings less than ten percent in electronics-based commodity is lying! Why? Moore's Law alone drives out at least 20% cost per year without procurement doing a thing!

So how do you prove value in supply chain? PPV? Negotiated savings?

Nope. I'd submit anything related to material purchase cost reductions is fraught with problems. Believability tops the list. So where should you focus? Remember, it's about cash. Do you recall financial accounting and the current ratio? Compare current assets to current liabilities and voila, you can determine the health of a company —at least from an asset management point of view. And what is the most important asset? CASH. And as an SCM practitioner, you spend the heck out of your company's cash and in some cases lose it (see above). What if you were able to demonstrate in real, verifiable numbers that your strategies were saving cash. Think you might get the attention of the top of your business? You bet!

Okay, let's talk about the concept of the cash conversion cycle and its three elements—inventory, receivables, and payables. Go recruit your friends in finance to help you (You'll need them later anyway.), and ask them to tell you how many days of the three elements your business has. They don't know how to do it or you don't have a friend in finance? No worries, figure it out yourself. First determine your daily COGS (cost of goods sold). If you're a public company, that's easy enough—it's on the income statement (See, there is a reason you took financial accounting.) Find total COGS and divide that number by the number of days covered by the statement (quarterly = 90 days, yearly = 365, you got it, right?). The computed result is the daily value of COGS.

Now compare the daily value of COGS to the total value of the three elements of the cash conversion cycle (found on the balance sheet). Divide the value (of receivables, inventory, and payables) by a daily COGS, and you have the number of days in each of the three elements of the cash conversion cycle. Now add the two asset categories together (that's receivables and inventory) and subtract the liability (payables) from the result. You will likely get a positive number higher than 50. Which means your business has greater than 50 days of cash tied up. And who tied it up?

Go look in the mirror. It's YOU, the supply chain practitioner. Not that it's a bad thing—it is, after all, your job . You've got to have inventory to sell stuff, right? But do you need so much? Can you drive strategies to lower it? Of course, and you already are, but it's masked as inventory reduction plans, not cash liberation plans.

And how about payables? Can you effect a change there? Why not? If you extend your payment terms, you free up cash, right? Go for it .

The cool part is you can demonstrate actual cash savings in perpetuity as a result of simply stating your strategies in terms of freeing up cash and taking deserved credit for it . Every day of cash freed up by reducing your cash conversion cycle is money in the bank, and your executives will love it! If you figure a 5% cost of capital against the value of cash you will free up, you've got some real money there, right? AND you are not faking it. (This is where you MUST get your financial friends to agree with the value you created and corroborate your figures.) This is REAL money!

So, you want to cut 10% out of your business right away? Extend payables by ten days and see what happens, or reduce your inventory, or do both. Not only will you save your enterprise cash today, it's the gift that keeps on giving! Good luck and go liberate some cash.

* * *

George Bordon
Vice President, Procurement & Supply Management
Clarke American
gbordon@sbcglobal.net

I'm the VP of Procurement at Clarke American. We produce checks for, and offer related products to, financial institution customers, providing world-class service to those customers, acting as a "brand behind the brand" to deepen and grow their relationship with the financial institution. For the past seven years our procurement operation has been going through a transformation.

Seven years ago, we had a limited number of defined procurement processes. Supply management was left to the various organizations of the company, so we had a pretty decentralized procurement operation. Our journey began with CEO and Senior Executive Leadership Team buy-in for organizational and process change. They felt that procurement has to align with the business, so they added a VP Procurement & Supply Management to the team.

First, we established category management, bringing in strategic procurement professionals to blend with internal, high-performing associates who had great familiarity with the business. We identified our most significant opportunities and segmented our suppliers based on a combination of total spend and relative strategic value or criticality to the business. This gave us our initial focus.

Over three years, category management, combined with supplier consolidation, the establishment of supplier scorecard metrics, engagement in a consortium, and early work on supplier development saved cumulatively 19 % of our annual spend.

But after three years, we began to see a "plateau effect" in our cumulative savings as the low-, and even medium-hanging, fruit had been picked. We'd moved from "breakthrough" to "continuous improvement". The team continued to deliver savings, but the annual contribution had decreased to about half the prior rate. So we increased efforts in value management, using cross-functional teams from Clarke American and the supplier to attack costs and eliminate waste across the supply chain (our process, their process, or in between). This allowed us to reduce our costs—even where we had no real leverage.

To add additional value, we used this approach to engage suppliers in new product and service development and to address customer satisfaction issues. Keeping suppliers keenly aware of our end customer is a critical success factor for us. We began to align our approaches more closely with the Malcolm Baldrige quality framework as well. These new efforts brought more savings. We also began to hold quarterly reviews with our business stakeholders and their financial analysts, which helped maintain alignment and gained sponsorship for our initiatives. After five years, cumulative savings had reached 24.9% of annual spend.

While accelerating savings again, we still had not reached the rate of savings capture seen in the early years. So we went to work more heavily on developing our key strategic supplier relationships. In Year 6, we provided engagement workshops to include suppliers on our key company project teams. This helped us work more effectively together and delivered additional value. We also stepped up our supplier recognition program for outstanding suppliers, creating an effective incentive for other suppliers to improve. That got us 3.7% savings, bringing the total over 6 years to approximately 29% of our annual spend.

Our next "breakthroughs" are in the development of strategic alliances or partnerships and an increased focus on logistics and supply chain. We're putting in place new tools to manage the five or ten most strategic supplier relationships on a strategic, tactical and operational level. These include the development of long-term joint relationship (change the business) goals and measures. We're on track to deliver another 5.2% savings in year 7 and to deploy new product offerings with our suppliers that will drive significant additional revenue and profit.

* * *

Quentin B. Samelson
Director, eSupply Strategy
Motorola
Quentin.B.Samelson@motorola.com

Here are five things I recommend you do to save money. This is the stuff you have to do when you walk in as a new materials manager and you want to make your mark:

The first two techniques work by understanding the key

cost drivers of a part. Whether a part is mechanical or electrical in nature, its cost is driven by some combination of materials used to make the part, the amount of labor required, the yield, and—sometimes—any intellectual property or capital expenditure involved.

1. Linear or Straight line analysis—To use this technique, you simply identify a group of similar parts, all the castings or tantalum chip capacitors, for instance. Look for the easily identified parameters that differentiate the parts from each other. For castings, this might be weight and the number of drilled holes; for tantalum chip caps, it will probably be case size, tolerance, voltage rating & capacitance value. Create a table of cost vs. those parameters, and plot them.

I remember doing this in 1991 when I had just started working at a medium-sized Electronic Manufacturing Services (EMS) Provider. We had about 20-30 part numbers in the same commodity. They varied in price from five cents to one dollar, and we couldn't figure out why, so we took all of them, the capacitance, tolerance and case size differences and plotted them and their cost against each other. Most of the difference in price was due to case size and tolerance; bigger case sizes mean more materials, therefore a higher price; and tighter tolerances mean lower yields, therefore also a higher price. But we found one part number that didn't "fit" with the others. We were buying a 5% tolerance part for less than the same part in a 20% tolerance, but tighter (tolerance) is supposed to be more expensive! Of course, that meant that we were paying way too much for the 20% part.

How does something like this occur? When you are doing engineering buys, or starting a new program, if you are buying a small quantity of a 20% part, you might get a high price, such as 50¢. But your first buy on the 5% part might be much more substantial—say $50,000. So we paid something like 30¢ for it and created this discrepancy. It's easy to get locked into the system. The next time, if the buyer buys the 50¢ item for just 45¢, he thinks he's a hero—even though he's paying way too much for it!

Unless the commodity manager is watching, you can end up paying whatever the market will bear, for no reason.

So it's important to find the key characteristic that drives price, do a plot, and see which parts don't end up on the straight line.

As another example, take castings. Most will start with a price that is the weight of iron or aluminum in the casting, so a two-pound casting should cost roughly twice the one-pound casting. To that the manufacturer will add the cost of drilling holes & finishing. But on average if you buy five different castings of different weights, you should see at least a rough correlation between price and weight . On a plot of price vs. weight, the different products should be more or less on a straight line (and you should be able to identify why specific part numbers are not on that straight line). Know the reason for the price, because lots of times you find no good reason.

(Bare, unassembled) PC boards are another great example. Suppliers have to think in terms of yield based on whatever master size they use -- say 2 x 3 feet. Their cost depends on how many of your product will fit into that master size. Another supplier uses a different master configuration (maybe 2.5 x 2.5 feet). Even though both of these master sizes are close to the same surface area (6 square feet vs. 6.25 square feet), the number of individual boards that will fit onto the master can be significantly different -- especially if they are a somewhat unusual shape. But the value to us, the customer, doesn't vary according to the manufacturer's yield. For the same kind of PC board, the cost to us ought to be the same per square inch. So it is valuable to look at cost per square inch on a category like PC boards.

2. Commodity volume buying—Simply look for subcategories that could be purchased at a single, unified price. Chip resistors and capacitors that share primary characteristics (size, voltage spec, tolerance , etc.) should be the same price, at least for most values. Generally speaking, there is no significant difference in materials, labor, or capital investment between a 10 Ohm resistor and a 47,000 Ohm resistor. If the supplier makes millions of these in different values, why should you pay different prices for different values? Not only that, but you should use the entire volume to leverage your negotiations, not the individual vol-

umes by different part numbers. Of course, this only seems to work well in very homogeneous commodities.

3. Frequently people don't really recognize the cost of holding inventory. Check to see what kind of turns you are getting on purchased parts. I've often found a situation where the company gets, for instance, ten turns overall on purchased parts, but too much inventory is tied up in A parts (which are supposed to turn quickly, with only a week or two on hand). I have a really simple technique to cut down on inventory of A parts. The idea is to simply mathematically "float to the top" that small number of part numbers which (a) could be managed aggressively for inventory down to a week or so; and which (b) currently are over their limit, and (c) which account for the greatest amount of excessive inventory dollars.

The process is fairly simple in concept. Essentially, you run an ABC report, with the parts sorted in descending dollar sequence for parts to buy in the next 3-6 mos, and you add one more piece of information: current on-hand inventory levels. The ABC report gives you a great tool to segregate parts by the number of dollars they consume per week. Understanding consumption per week, and on-hand inventory levels, will let you do great things with the A parts, which are usually no more than 5-6% of the part numbers you work with, but 80% of the dollars. With a small population to work with, you can do a little micromanaging. Sometimes you'll even find that the first 1% of part numbers represents 50% of the dollars, so a very small number of parts can swing a lot of inventory.

The goal is to set a guideline. If you only have 50 parts to manage, couldn't you manage them on a week or so inventory? Have a supplier bring parts in a day at a time. Most companies don't actively manage it, but I would force the buyers to each manually manage 2-5 part numbers. It's part of their metrics; they are measured weekly or monthly on how skinny they can manage these parts. It works like this: You are supposed to have, let's say, 1.5 wks; you look in the ABC report, look at the on-hand, so you know what 1 week's worth. And if there is too much, make sure you don't get any more . It's a routine—on Monday mornings, I would pull out the report and review it buyer by buyer, looking for which A parts there are too many of. What I was really looking for was the value of the excess on hand. That was the value of the quantity over the amount we needed to keep operations going. (One of the tricks with this technique is to come up with a definition that everyone understands meaning "too much on hand for current needs.") If we define 1.5 weeks as a reasonable operating quantity for A parts, and that represents 15,000 parts, but one part number (worth $10 each) has 30,000 on hand, we have $150,000 in excess on hand. I would allow buyers to compensate for parts that they intentionally were running a little "fat" by running others a little "skinny"—just look at the bottom line. If there was a significant dollar value of excess on hand, we would have a little chat with the buyer to identify any problems they were having and encourage them to work the excess down.

Most buyers figure it out pretty quickly. We had one buyer running big, bulky parts with surface shipment over 1,400 miles. He hit 50 turns. He didn't hit it every week, but he was running 45-50 turns just like clockwork; there was almost no investment—it was great.

It's a simple concept. Find the A parts, keep refreshing the A parts, and basically measure the actual quantity on hand of A parts vs. desired inventory. Unfortunately, many of the MRP/ERP systems I've encountered define Excess or Surplus as "the difference between total quantity on hand (plus on order) and the total forecasted requirements." In other words, the definition they use ignores time and just totals up all forecasted supply and compares that to all forecasted demand. That is useful only for avoiding obsolescence. In a continuous manufacturing environment, you need to shrink the timeframe down to the next week or so. Do I have everything on hand I need to build today's requirements? Will I have everything I need tomorrow to build tomorrow's requirements? People are used to thinking in that way. All this technique does is look at the opposite side of the question: What do I have on hand today that I don't need today, tomorrow or even this week? Why is it there? Let's make sure that if I have three weeks' worth of an expensive A part, that I don't receive any more until I've just about used up that three weeks' worth.

At any rate, this sort of quick analysis can often double turns. And if you can move turns from, say, 8 to 16, that's equivalent to a percentage cost savings on the part. (This depends on the holding cost you assign to inventory, which includes the cost of money, insurance, labor, cost of floor space, etc.) At a 12% carrying cost, going from 8 to 16 turns (equivalent to reducing from 6 weeks on hand to only 3 weeks) is the same as a 0.75% cost reduction on the parts themselves.

4. I often find no standards , or inconsistently applied standards, for setting up part lead times. For instance, one line may be running all parts due on Monday, the lines all due for Friday production, which leaves only three days of lead time. That means usually at the beginning of the week we were short of something. We were underplanning, whereas the focus of planning on Monday was way too much. The critical factor is individual lead times—receiving lead time, inspection lead time—and they all need to be aligned.

Production Planners often employ different strategies for scheduling production, without realizing that this can result in inconsistent materials due dates in the purchasing area. For example:

Perhaps we need to build 10,000 pieces of Product A per week, so planner 1 loads an order for 10,000 pieces due on each Friday (even though we actually try to build 20,00 pieces a day).

Perhaps we need to build 25,000 pieces of Product B per week, in several different varieties, so planner 2 loads specific orders for each variety for each day— 5,000 pieces on Monday, 5,000 pieces on Tuesday, etc.

Perhaps we need to build 4,000 pieces of Product C per week, but they ship out on Wednesdays and it only takes one day of production time, so planner 3 loads an order for 4000 pieces each Monday.

If each product has the same manufacturing lead times loaded (perhaps 1 day assembly, 1 day final test, 1 day pack & ship, 1 day staging):

The materials requirements for Product C will pop out on the previous Wednesday.

The materials requirements for Product B will pop out with 5,000 due the previous Wednesday, 5,000 the prevous Tuesday, 5,000 the previous Monday, 5,000 the Friday two weeks ago, and 5,000 on the Thursday two weeks ago.

The materials requirements for Product A will pop out on the Monday of the current week.

(We might also add a couple of days for receiving/put-away/incoming inspection.) I've encountered scenarios like this repeatedly. Of course, you probably already noticed that the materials requirements for product A are much later than the equivalent requirements for product B, even though they are both being produced at a steady daily rate. Product A's manufacturing line actually needs parts starting on the previous Wednesday, but the parts will be scheduled to be available on Monday of the current week. If Product A and Product B share parts, product A will steal parts from product B, shutting down product B's manufacturing line sporadically. When product B checks their planning parameters, they will all look ok, so they'll blame the supplier, blame purchasing, etc. The whole operation's planning parameters need to be consistent. Otherwise you'll waste time & energy chasing shortages that are self-caused!

5. Dollar Days

Actually, I don't use this as much in materials management as with customers. It's a technique I call "Dollar Days". I came up with it when we had a huge problem at an EMS; it was hard to decide which past dues to do first. So I use the time value of money; multiply the number of days past due times the dollars past due—that creates a very big number. Its so simple; you prioritize 10 days and 1M late, over 1 day and 2M late, and you rapidly start to fix the most egregious past due situations. We dropped in three months from 30M dollar days to 3M dollar days. Customers loved it. We simply focused attention on the one or two really bad items, then the next couple—it's a nice progression. It gave us a feeling of control. Plus it's easy to pull this information out of the order entry system; pull all past due orders, take the dollars past due, multiply by days past dues. Do this first thing in the morning, and make sure you are working on the worst ones.

* * *

Overhead

Take a good careful look at how products are costed in the overhead area. When volumes increase, overhead should not proportionately increase, because really, volumes are independent of traditional cost accounting overhead protocol.

Lean manufacturing, or kaizen projects, should yield at least a 3 to 1 return for supplier development engineer involvement, either in better quality and higher throughput per person—efficiency —or in reduced work in process, which is cash flow, particularly for small suppliers.

* * *

Ken McGuire, Massachusetts-based
lean pioneer, MEACCAPECD

Go paperless!

I call it the electronic kanban thing. It's not software, it's a network. If you think about the days when we used to get pink notes telling us we had a message, and we could always blame whoever wrote the note, well, then we got voice mail. You no longer can complain that you never got it—you can't miss it, and you can't complain that someone didn't get it right, because it is what it is.

What this is, is an inexpensive Signum network, and a network kanban for small and medium sized cos, costs $250 per seat and $10 per supplier. Essentially DataCraft bought the excess capacity on the premier network in supply chain and then resold it with some kanban features on it that allow small and medium-sized companies to have a network more secure than they could afford to buy and more reliable than they could afford themselves. Salesforce.com is the model. The barrier to entry is zero. You can't afford not to try it.

You save all the costs of transactions. Let's be generous and say it's $35 for each purchasing transaction. Immediately that's the payback. But what Signum enables you to do is go paperless. Have bar code on the cell, where your parts person simply barcodes a signal into the PC, that goes on the Internet and posts on your supplier. And there are huge savings. This enables a small company to multiply its transactions geometrically. So for a company that gets 20 deliveries per day, has been trying to do it with faxes, now we are talking about doing 20 per day, or more, with smaller containers and more locations, and it's effortless. All of sudden you are now able to do 30 times per day with ease and go to next step—the invoice—and the next step, put it on credit card.

DJ Ortho in California is using this solution. I participated in the design of the DataCraft product. We put in it in four different kinds of industries—basic industrial, then medical products, where it is a tool for managing their supply chain and distribution. DJ Ortho, for instance, dispenses braces at clinics; the software manages replenishment. Each time a brace is removed from the cabinet, it is barcoded and a replacement arrives the next day. The solution is also being used in automotive—not with the auto assemblers, curiously enough, but with the suppliers to the suppliers of auto assemblers, two levels down the chain, where Toyota never gets. They are also in aerospace (Danaher).

We can compete with China.

We still have two strong advantages against China. First, they are missing a sense of customer management. Our edge is that we can get extremely close to our customers.

And second, they are not good at inventory management. They think like we did in the 1940s, "if you need some, you buy a year's worth." They're getting smarter, but right now they're not very smart.

* * *

Payment terms can get you 2-4% savings if you can give the supplier better cash flow. If he knows you are going to pay his invoice, preferably electronically, in less than 30 days without prompting, that saves him a lot of paperwork, hours of cross-matching of invoices to shipping documents, etc., and that's labor costs. So many customers are extending their payment terms that suppliers are happy to encourage quicker receivables by offering discounts.

* * *

Dave Nelson,
Vice President, Global Supply Management
Delphi Corporation
(former head of purchasing at John Deere
 and Honda of America)

Consortium buying—we have participated in lots of consortium buying, but they don't work very well. For all the right logic they ought to work, and maybe somebody could make it work if they are big enough, like IBM, but the longest running one was one out of Buffalo. I talked with different people that were in it, and they all were less than thrilled about it. What's interesting is if you take a company that up to now didn't do consortium buying among plants and divisions—if you don't do it with plants and divisions where you could save 30-40% between what one plant pays and another pays—it's not so likely you are going to go head over heels for the concept. Consortiums are extremely difficult because you often buy different things— one group likes one kind and another likes another kind. Whether you realize it or not, every company has a culture about the things they use, and not just a culture in things they use, but the way they go about buying them. There is a great problem in alignment, and it's just more work than anybody wants to put into it.

We tried at Deere a consortium with three other companies for steel and plastics and other things, but it didn't work. One guy laid his job on the line and the number 2 guy quit his main job, had a percentage deal with it, tried for a year, and it just wouldn't work, even with that much attention, and he's already a wealthy guy. Somebody will be successful some day, maybe IBM, but they will have to have a huge buy of many things on their computer that you can just plug into and buy. And if you want to add your own things, it has to fit into their contract so you get a better deal. I am satisfied that when somebody figures that out and gets it rolling, it could be like Monopoly because they will be able to buy stuff like Wal-Mart—if you get big enough, you can do it successfully, particularly if you have a plug-in system. One of the key secrets to success is to somehow interface part numbers and methodologies to the standards, so if we don't want to change the part number for that pen, we use a configurator. Won't work unless there is a plug-in system like a web system to do the ordering easily. IBM is the closest to being able to do it. This could make somebody extremely wealthy, but nobody wants to spend the time.

* * *

Garry Berryman
Former head of procurement at Harley-Davidson and AMD, now CPO at Sara Lee

1. Develop a multiyear supplier purchase commitment strategy that enables a supplier to plan for investments in their operations which yield cost improvements that can be passed on to their customer.

Example: A supplier of very sophisticated chemical delivery systems made an investment in a low cost area to expand their footprint. They had to create an infrastructure and staff it to expand the scope. The investment that supplier made in their global footprint was only enabled through the confidence that it was their business with their customer to lose—it's not a free ride. They had a multiyear contract with a performance commitment on quality, cost, and technology. Should they have fallen off the map, they would have lost the business.

When the supplier put forth the business case to expand, the customer worked through a multiyear, minimum three years. Most companies want a three-year pay-back, but most often suppliers want longer, say five, but if you can't make it pay in three you have to question whether it was the right thing to do. That forces the top of the company to be in that decision process—it's not just a transaction any longer. And when you get the top involved, there are better commitments, access to recourse, and the whole relationship is redefined. There are opportunities you can't see in a transactional environment .

There is a price change here because the cost reduction has to be substantial. As a customer you expect cost reductions from the lower cost far greater than 10% return, for three years probably a 30 % reduction. These savings are worth going after.

But you have to have the best and brightest people who get the business models, who know how to put together a business case that delivers value for both parties—it's low risk, high level thinking. That's the beauty of it, it's very, very low risk because all the due diligence is done ahead of pulling the lever, and bright people, once they know the solution, will deliver the details.

2. Integrate the supplier personnel, including the supplier's executive management, into the product and process development roadmaps. Through this forward look the "Know-how" and technical expertise can be leveraged toward the roadmap initiatives.

The roadmap thing, it's low-hanging fruit. If you go to almost any supplier, describe your customers technology or product road map, 80% of them won't be able to do that because they are also operating from a transactional perspective. The reason they can't do it is their customer doesn't see the value of it, and so the supplier doesn't pursue it. In a lot of cases, companies don't have clear roadmaps. It's hard to do product or process roadmaps when you force the customer to articulate what it looks like. But we've done that with our own customers. We asked them for roadmaps, and we in turn supplied one. For a three-year time frame, by product line by process, we want to look at what are their investments. This is something the design and development, engineering community cannot do without help.

Although it's usually an ad hoc picture that hasn't been formalized, we force it to be written down. Then ask the question, what's the roadmap, can we develop, then why, then do a value proposition; if you have a map, you will understand the technical resources needed, then can tie the suppliers' technology with it and put cost targets on it. Once there is a cost target on it, ask what the targeted cost on this process is vs. whatever it is replacing. With a target cost, it's possible to frame the engineering thinking. And that's where the money's at.

3. Quality improvements that produce zero waste. Eliminating all quality waste will provide significant productivity efficiencies.

For every dollar invested, we got six back, but to do that we had to frame it in an environment of zero tolerance. That whole idea of zero tolerance is easy to understand – it didn't take a lot of explaining. When you talk about six sigma and black belts and ppm, they always have a margin of tolerance, and when people see that, they have a tendency to expand it, so we simply have put forward zero tolerance in 4 areas. One is in true quality capability of your quality leadership, adherence to standards and specs in the execution of your product or service. We were managing very complex, customized products in a global environment, dealing with a lot of PhDs., mighty smart people. The zero tolerance concept, for return of 6 to 1, was an easy proposition, but they had to know how product was performing in customer environment—the return in people or systems in quality is 6 to 1.

So the first task is to know your quality environment— how capable are my quality leaders, what licenses, what certifications, what demonstrated capability, and look at your output quality level. All due diligence will demonstrate the quality foundation, and then you simply go in and find the 6 to 1 opportunity.

4. Hire the best and brightest purchasing professionals that understand both the commercial and technical aspects of the business and resulting relationships with suppliers. You will have to pay nationally competitive compensation, but do not make the mistake of being penny wise and pound foolish.

Where do I find these people? Those folks find purchasing because they see the capabilities that most can't. Like Richter and Nelson saw the business leverage that nobody else could, they come with the fundamentals and strong leadership that enables them to be enormously influential. The influence factor comes through the capability of the individual to see the whole thing. I do it though finances—you've got to see the whole business, because it's all around influence.

* * *

Quentin.Samelson@motorola.com

Conduct an inspection tour of the stockroom, receiving dock, etc. One of the things that experienced operations people do is a walkthrough, looking for:

*Stacks of FedEx (or other airfreight) labels. If many are found in the stockroom, airfreight is probably being used inappropriately—too much. This can be an easy way to cut operating costs quickly.

I observed this at two different jobs... unopened boxes, still with their airfreight label, sitting in the raw materials warehouse. Once in a while it could happen because of a last-minute schedule change (what was urgent yesterday is suddenly not urgent today), but if you see very many instances like this it may be due to:

Either a buyer or a supplier mistakenly applying airfreight as the standard shipping method, because one shipment last year (of that part number, or from that supplier) was urgent and had to be sent via airfreight. All it takes is for the buyer to tell a distributor "Make sure you ship it airfreight" one time, and the customer service person at the supplier may code it as the default shipping method.

Buyer/planners sometimes get hooked on the fact that airfreight is easy to track. It gets tiresome when people ask, "Where's that shipment?" and you can't answer. So they may tend toward air freight just to get the easy tracking. However, it's really not very hard to get tracking service with small parcel shipment these days. So you don't have to go all the way to air freight to be able to track a shipment.

Conflict of metrics... The buyer may be measured only on part cost, which may push him or her to a somewhat less reliable supplier. The cost of freight often ends up on the manufacturing line, or at least is not part of the buyer's scorecard. It can get even worse if the buyer is measured on his or her suppliers' on-time performance. Then the buyer is incented to bring in the cheapest parts, on schedule . . . but doesn't get penalized if freight costs are too high!

Unrealistic manufacturing schedules in the MRP system. This happens when you have multiple people trying to use the same (limited) resources. They'll drive materials in so that materials shortages can't stop production, but they're all scheduling a constrained resource so the parts just sit. This can also be caused by out-of-control sales commitments or customer service people jockeying for position for their customers.

* Dusty boxes, period, in the stockroom. If materials are sitting around long enough to gather dust, there's something wrong with the way they are being brought in. Even in those cases where it made economic sense to buy a large lot of parts, dusty boxes indicate lack of activity. If you see dusty boxes on the main thoroughfare of your stockroom, you have slow-moving materials interfering with the efficient operation of the stockroom. Consolidate them and move them someplace away from the action—or get rid of them.

* Storage methods. Are they efficient? Is there the possibility of losing parts (which often occurs when parts are stored in part-number sequence, or with multiple part numbers in the same location)?

Working at smaller operations, I observed that it was perfectly understandable to start out storing parts in part-number sequence. But if the operation grows very much, that becomes completely inappropriate. It seems like this is very much like the "how to boil a frog" story. People just don't notice that things are getting out of control because they're not using random storage. At one company, people would force additional containers of a part number into position when there really wasn't any room left. Other containers would get shoved to the shelf behind. Parts would "wander" up and down the length of the shelving, and of course they could never be found when they were needed. So we'd buy more—and then have to write off the "lost" parts when they were found again!

How far materials move from the dock door to the receiving area to the stockroom, and how they move (by hand, by conveyor, etc.). I've seen some areas that would curdle your blood.

At the last plant where I was actually a materials manager, we originally had lift trucks picking up pallets of materials and moving them all over the warehouse to put them away. Even with RF barcode equipment & random stores, it was inefficient. We replaced that with a conveyor system that moved all the small boxes automatically to three different areas, based on the velocity of the parts. Fast-moving parts went to a set of flow racks, slow-moving parts went to an area where we could really pack parts in densely, and medium-moving parts went to a set of shelves. The bulky items that had to be moved by lift trucks were put the closest to the receiving dock. That meant that the guys running the lift trucks were able to operate much more efficiently. They just moved full pallets of bulky items, instead of trying to move boxes, etc.

I visited a facility (that had actually been featured on the cover of *Modern Materials Handling!*) where the stores area was down a long, long, long aisle from the dock door, and they didn't even use lift trucks. Every shipment that was received had to be moved by hand, at least the length of a football field. It just made my blood boil! These were parts that were very inexpensive to manufacture (in Asia), but the U.S. distributor was expending expensive American labor just to put them away.

A lot of the most progressive ideas can be applied nearly everywhere, but it's often not practical to push them to the limit. (Of course, pushing them to the limit is what people often expect, based on popular concepts of zero inventory or JIT, or lean manufacturing.) Running a facility in south

Texas, far from the suppliers of electronic components and the manufacturers of mechanical parts, it is foolhardy to run a plant on zero inventory. I found out —the hard way —that it wasn't even smart to keep two days' worth of parts in the stockroom during the winter, because a good winter storm could shut down transportation for half a week. But we still were able to apply the concepts of JIT and zero inventory to our situation. So with each idea you have to look at the underlying concept & decide how it can be applied, and how far it should be applied, in a particular situation. We absolutely had a locked stockroom in Austin, TX , (inside a larger stores area) because the parts were so valuable that we were robbed once at gunpoint. (Another time there was an attempted burglary that was foiled by the cage!).

I've seen line-side storage implemented well, and I've also seen it used without much discipline on the shop floor, resulting in poor control, terrible inventory accuracy, and other issues. So I think you have to fit the solution to the problem and to the characteristics of the facility/ operation. Line-side deliveries (and supplier-operated inventory hubs) are a great idea for the customer, but they cost the suppli- ers real money, don't they? So the supplier has to be able to cost-justify them based on the volume of business they do with the customer. All these ideas need to pass the com- monsense test.

It's really easy to get seduced by a particular idea or tool, whether it is JIT or SPC or six sigma, and forget that they are all just tools, they are not the goal. The goal is profits, or lower costs, or improved productivity—and a good supply chain or materials manager will evaluate how various tools can be applied to achieve the goal. We've all seen the results when people start to treat the tool or tech- nique as the goal! (In the early '90s, it seems like I had a visit or call at least once a month from a distributor who wanted to give me near-infinite inventory turns—at a cost adder of 5-8%. It sounded attractive until I calculated that even going to 50 or 100 turns would only save us 1.5-2%. (This is where that inventory spreadsheet came from.) High inventory turns are wonderful, but in and of themselves they don't produce a positive business result.

* * *

Eddy Guarascio
Manager, Global Procurement
Medrad
eguarascio@medrad.com

Gross margin improvement

In order to support its historic and continued growth, MEDRAD, Inc. started a Gross Margin Improvement initiative that has saved money and uncovered new opportunities. An executive offsite brainstorming session in Fall 2003 led MEDRAD to identify a companywide need for improved gross margin beyond traditional cost reduction programs. Gross Margin Improvement was targeted as a "Top 12" corporate objective . . . #8 in 2004 and #5 in 2005. A higher gross margin was needed to invest in the infrastructure and future of MEDRAD. The long-term objective was to improve gross margin percentage by 5% between 2003 and 2008. The specific objective for 2004 was to identify and implement programs that would generate a minimum of $2M of incremental gross margin ($1M through channel management and pricing and $1M through supply chain improvements). A model of the program was communicated throughout MEDRAD.

We started working internally within Procurement to reduce "total systems costs" (related to MEDRAD's spend) by a minimum of $10M by CY 2008 and drawing in more partners, looking for big opportunities and following the 80/20 rule. The "supplier cost reduction" segment was billed as "Project 1008" (reduce baseline spend by $10M by 2008) and communicated to our supply base. The project is time-phased and intended to target MEDRAD internal productivity enhancements and joint projects with key supply partners.

For example, MEDRAD worked with two plastic injection molders to implement new five-year agreements with moderate annual cost downs commensurate with Project 1008 objectives. MEDRAD purchases over 150M plastic components annually. The agreement was structured to challenge the suppliers to abate cost increases and incorporate increasing 1% cost reductions per year growing to 5% by 2008. In parallel, MEDRAD committed to work closely with the suppliers to achieve cost down targets that grow more and more difficult each year. Generally, costs down below target were incentives to the suppliers. Our approach was to avoid specifics on a component-by-component basis; rather we let our suppliers go after opportunities. First target was material costs. Both suppliers were paying differing amounts for the same primary materials. They decided to collaborate, even though we were dual-sourcing the parts. With a five-year agreement, the significant MEDRAD spend and associated split of requirements was fully rationalized and clearly communicated to both suppliers. It was totally open from us to them and vice versa. Everyone recognizes that we're all in this together.

Supplier suggestions and shared savings

Recently, the Gross Margin Improvement initiative and Project 1008 was included as a hands-on workshop session at our annual Supplier Day. Further, based on recorded baseline savings, suppliers gained recognition at the event. During three breakout sessions, over 40 key suppliers, including many direct competitors, were educated on the program and brainstormed potential opportunities. Over 100 ideas were received and evaluated.

Day to day informal activities

MEDRAD also has a long-standing Value Improvement Program (VIP), a systematic way to generate project ideas, measure, track, and provide visibility of value improvements throughout MEDRAD Operations. The VIP Program promotes simple online recognition that results in designated rewards, periodic prize drawings, and an annual banquet. This program generated over $17M in savings and cost avoidance in CY 2004.

MEDRAD, INC. is a worldwide leading provider of medical devices and services that enable and enhance imaging procedures of the human body. Used in diagnostic imaging, MEDRAD's product offerings include a comprehensive line of vascular injection systems, magnetic resonance (MR) surface coils and accessory products, and equipment services. Total 2004 revenues were $343 million. MEDRAD is a

2003 recipient of the Malcolm Baldrige National Quality Award, the top honor a U.S. company can receive for quality and business excellence. The company's world headquarters is near Pittsburgh, Pennsylvania, in the United States. MEDRAD is a U.S. affiliate of Schering AG, Germany (NYSE:SHR). For more information, visit MEDRAD's web site at www.medrad.com.

* * *

Brian.Hietpas@harley-davidson.com
Product Category Manager – Material Cost

I am the category manager of material cost at Harley-Davidson. My department monitors material costs including metal markets, currencies, other raw materials and their impact on commercial cost reductions with suppliers. Harley has design engineers and purchasing engineers that design and agree on up front pricing with our suppliers. Once parts are in production, my group works with the supply base, ops purchasing, value engineering, and design engineering to continue to pull cost out of current parts. From a raw material standpoint, with recent steel and aluminum price escalations, the metal market analyst that works for me has seen an ever- increasing workload evaluating cost increases that our suppliers are coming to us with; he looks at what metals are doing to their margins and evaluates if price relief is warranted.

We have a lot of good initiatives ongoing:

1. Onsite supplier residents. We have suppliers that work at Harley, with Harley contractor badges that allow them to work up front with design engineers to make sure the design fits the suppliers' processes. About 20 suppliers are supported by "onsite residents." For instance, the harness supplier is on site, full-time. We have 4 Delphi engineers that supply ECMs, instrumentation and throttle bodies. They are engineers, not sales people, that become involved at the product development center from day 1. The intent is to save cost by designing components that fit their manufacturing processes and use the latest technology.

Another example would be a casting supplier resident that is onsite helping us design the geometry of castings to enable better mold tooling development.

2. Pay the sub-tier. Harley has many supply chains, such as for chrome parts and stampings houses. For the stamping house, for example, we buy chromed and unchromed stampings. With chrome stampings, the tier 1 supplier is the chrome house. When we buy a chromed stamping, we pay for the part but we actually buy two parts. We buy the chrome and the stamped portion. That way we aren't paying material markup for the stamping as it goes through the chrome house, so we have undone tiering relative to payments. In effect, we make two payments—one to the tier 1 supplier, the chrome house, and one to the tier 2 supplier, the stamping house. When we get the finished product —it is received under one part number, the final part number—then both suppliers get paid. How does this save money? Let's say the stamping is $10, and chroming is twenty additional dollars. If we were to just buy the part, all done from final supplier, that supplier would buy the $10 stamping part, bring it in as raw material, and they would put the raw material markup on it, approximately 20%, or $2. The $2 would be added to the $10, plus all their processing, $20 value add. In the "old days," the total would be $32, but now its $30. We're dealing with a little more paper, but it's well worth it.

3. In the development process, we have implemented a very stringent cost breakdown requirement on our suppliers. They are all required to break down our purchase price to a very minute level. In some cases, suppliers don't have the level that we ask for, but we feel that our purchasing engineers have to understand the cost drivers of all of the components they buy to make sure that the high cost drivers are being evaluated and hopefully reduced by design changes or process improvements.

4. Sequencing of parts from the supplier. Here's an example. We are building 150 Dyna motorcycles every day, and we sequence the seats so that the assembly line pulls up the cart and the parts are arranged all in sequence. Same thing with shocks. We order them by part number,

but they come in by our build sequence. For seats, for instance, we have five different types for a a particular model, but those five parts don't come in boxes by part number that then need to be separated and sorted on the line. The supplier sends them in according to our build schedule. The box goes directly to the line, and the operators have what they need in order. There is no in-house staging, which is extra inventory, extra handling, extra packaging, extra cost!

5. Returnable packaging

* * *

Chetan Patel
President, SMC
Somerset, Wisconsin
chetan@smcltd.com

What are key elements to the success of our company as we work with Respironics?

Looking at costs, and working very closely with the customer in the design phase.

We are small, with 45 molding machines, and we like this size. Because even though we are growing at a very nice rate, we don't want to spiral out of control. We have a special workforce that is basically home-grown—lots of in-house training, at high school, at vocational schools, also at university levels. Although the plastics industry has been very difficult in the last three years, we have grown considerably.

The key to our success is that we are a very engineering oriented, a very technology and engineering based company. We tend to buy the latest in equipment, process monitoring and automation, and that tends to attract a certain type of customer, such as Respironics. We try to understand the customer's need before we try to sell our services.

That's why at Respironics, a key customer, we have a Program Manager there three days per week. Our goal is to understand the true customer need, what is working, what could we help with, and only then we say "It's time to go to work on the quotation package." Then we give them a model of how it would work. Dave Butler at Respironics was very open in giving us access. Otherwise, it would have been difficult.

The other thing that was quite unique as the Respironics relationship developed is that they were very much interested in knowing how we do things, instead of just going through a quoting process. The people in procurement were people who had prior experience in plastics, and that has helped sharpen the focus.

People ask how involved we are in designing the product. We are very involved! When Respironics was talking to us about open book accounting, we said great, and then we said we would like a seat on their design team. We were not only going to provide design services, but we wanted to insure that the products incorporated good design-for-manufacturability, and that we could help speed up the entire design-and-build cycle.

As I mentioned, the Program Manager's role is to be sure we are communicating directly, and he is on site 2-3 days per week. In addition to that, we initially sent a design team from SMC with different disciplines—manufacturing engineers, process engineers, quality—during the design phase, although we hadn't yet been assigned the program. Their job was not just to help with design, but to watch manufacturability and cost issues. They also had access to any of the various engineers back in Somerset. It was a huge investment on SMC's part, but if we did that, it not only would help our customer, it would help us tremendously as we would face a lot fewer quality and manufacturing issues as we launched the program.

Our support for Respironics' new products is the biggest challenge over the next three years. As Respironics grows, my focus is to insure that SMC can continue to contribute to their success. We want to have the design, engineering and manufacturing capabilities that will keep them coming back for more. In the process, we want to insure for the benefit of our own organization, that we can do what Respironics, and companies like them, want done. In two words, that would be FASTER and BETTER.

* * *

Andy Collopy
Global Program Director, Procurement, BP plc
Andrew.Collopy@uk.bp.com

I worked with a global pharmaceuticals producer to improve their processes and save money. We applied lean manufacturing techniques to the Print area, including labels, leaflets and cartons. From time/value mapping, we discovered that 40% of a label or carton cost was driven by setup costs for tooling on the running machine at the supplier. In a highly complex area with thousands of stock keeping units (SKUs) the constant switching of tooling to meet demand-driven short runs was adding significant cost into the print price per thousand due to setup times. So the company used Master Black Belts who worked with print suppliers to drive down the setup times and reduce the print cost per thousand by 20%.

The Black Belts identified solutions to reduce setup time: a) a closer collaboration between the customer scheduling and supplier planning areas to optimize print runs b) they worked with the setup engineers to remove waste, reducing setup times from 4hrs to 2.5hrs c) they worked with Marketing to reduce the number of part numbers, colors, specification profiles etc.

In another project, the team applied Six Sigma statistical controls to a medical device which required highly accurate plastic components in order to give an exact respiratory treatment dosage. Deviations against the tight specification in the plastic components were resulting in excessive scrapping and increased costs. We used Six Sigma principles at the supplier to reduce variation in the process, resulting in a step change in components meeting specification. The reduction of scrap material and administration associated with managing scrapping, replacement stock expediting etc. delivered 30% improvement in scrap.

The quality problem was on the dispensing components within the medical device. The exact dosing requirement was the issue because it required a virtually variance-free specification which was not normal practice within the plastics industry and which caused a lot of the components to not meet what was a very tough specification. Six Sigma helped the plastics supplier significantly improve their specification tolerances to meet the required spec.

Here's one more example:

The supply into a pharmaceutical site of a regulated active ingredient was suffering from a 30% quality reject rate with knock-on effects on service and cost. Management was concerned that supply would not be able to keep pace with expected increases in sales. Procurement discussed the issues with the company's receiving site and agreed to use the site Lean Sigma resource to investigate. Working closely with the supplier, a team baselined the current process and used Lean Sigma tools to analyze and identify areas for improvement. As a result, the reject rate batch yield improved by 6%. By eliminating the need for rework and wasted time, the effective plant capacity rose by 150 %, thus securing Assurance of Supply for increased demand. In addition, process and supply chain improvements delivered over 20% cost reduction within 18 months.

Consider these three cost-cutting approaches:

1. Low Cost Country Sourcing – a palatable option

In some industries the move to LCCS has been slow due to high internal resistance born out of concerns over product quality, the high degree of regulation of that particular industry or reluctance to change. This can be seen in the pharmaceutical and oil & gas industries whereby today LCCS is only a small proportion of the total spend with third party suppliers.

One solution to this resistance is to actively engage a reputable, strategic third party supplier working in partnership to deliver a LCCS solution. The two parties work hand in hand identifying, qualifying and managing a LCCS supplier to deliver the product at the required specification. The strategic partner manages the LCCS supplier to ensure quality, service and assurance of supply integrity whilst cost benefits are gain-shared between the two parties.

This approach has been explored in the Catalyst commodity area at an oil and gas supermajor where sourcing focus has moved to explore potential sources of catalysts in the Far East instead of the traditional sourcing markets of Europe or the US. Whilst initial indications highlighted that the cost base could be reduced by some 30%, it was difficult to convince internal stakeholders that a move to a LCCS supplier was the right strategy given the perceived risks of supply from such a supplier, which could result in significant costs to the business should anything go wrong, such as out of specification material or poor service delivery.

This classic dilemma of high cost saving potential vs. business risk is commonplace in most Procurement organisations. The solution in this case was to begin discussions with a recognised US based catalyst provider about catalyst sourcing possibilities in LCCS areas. The incentive from the recognised provider's viewpoint is continuity of business— the customer not eventually moving the business away to an LCCS provider and cost benefit gain-share. For the oil and gas supermajor, the benefits are numerous: cost savings of 15% in this case, easy implementation due to the material being managed through a reputable source, therefore removing the internal resistance obstacles, and LCCS experience that can be applied in other commodity areas.

2. Strategic Sourcing – Beyond Tier 1

In the last 5yrs, the vast majority of Procurement organisations have embarked upon some form of Strategic Sourcing initiative. The categorization of spend into meaningful commodity, geographic or business areas has allowed Procurement organisations to manage the supply base in a structured, strategic way that has delivered significant value benefits both in $ terms as well as qualitative benefits such as risk reduction or quality improvements.

This Strategic Sourcing approach has been enabled to a certain extent by technology. The growth of eSourcing in the last 3-5yrs is probably one of the best examples of B2B interaction of the Internet age. For companies that have driven eSourcing uptake in their organisations, especially with tools such as eAuctions, savings delivery has averaged in the region of 20%.

This success is phenomenal and has been one of the

major influences in Procurement as an entity raising its profile at the boardroom table. However, in the vast majority of Procurement organisations that have taken the Strategic Sourcing approach, the sphere of influence has only been as far as their direct Level 1 suppliers.

Suppliers beyond Tier 1 are seldom managed by Procurement professionals. They are seen as somewhat out of bounds or the responsibility of their direct supplier to get right. In fact, the reality is that Tier 2 and beyond suppliers are within bounds and not only that, they are probably being poorly managed by your direct supplier.

While I worked in pharmaceuticals, I participated in a number of Engineering, Procurement and Construction (EPC) projects for significant new builds. Rather than leave the procurement of goods and services to the nominated EPC provider, the company actively got involved in the Procurement activity. Ultimately the end bill came to our company, so this made absolute sense. In most cases, the Procurement approach from the EPC provider was basic and "meeting budget" focused. It was the old adage of "if it's not your own money, you don't spend it like your own money."

We were recognised in our industry for Strategic Sourcing and eSourcing expertise & we used this expertise in working with its EPC provider on each of the new build project subelements to derive the greatest value through eAuctions and preferred deal usage. The $ benefits were significant, often resulting in projects meeting or coming in under budget which otherwise would have been overspent.

This success led our company to investigate influencing the supply base beyond Tier 1 in other areas such as resin purchase on plastic bottles or hotel prices within travel agency deals.

3. Apply Lean and Six Sigma principles and techniques with the supply base.

* * *

annielamb@msn.com

Anne Curry, former LLBean Inventory Specialist for International Retail Operations, says:

It's a New Year, so clean up your act!
An Asian tradition

At midnight of the Chinese New Year a gong is struck 108 times. The gong absolves everyone of all 108 sins (don't know where that number comes from). Then, everyone pays off all debts, purges unneeded stuff, cleans drawers, files, closets (houses are quite small, and there is no storage space) so the new year can begin with a fresh slate—new, clean energy. How long does this take? China, Singapore, Taiwan shut down for a week. Japan is getting more and more Westernized and doesn't officially close for a week anymore. But the hoopla/de-cluttering/celebration lasts a week. The goal is to let go of the past so you can move forward with uncluttered energy. The word "clutter" comes from the Middle English word "clotter," which means coagulate.

* * *

Chad Moody
Ford Motor Company
Cost Optimization
cmoody1@ford.com

Design is where the money starts to build up, so if you do a teardown, you're going to find some interesting things happening in your products. Or you can actually compare your products to the competition's.

One way is to completely disassemble and research the costs on every component —yours and competition's. Estimates of value analysis/value engineering savings range from 20-30% on products that have not been examined before. Purchasing must be involved on the reverse-engineering team so that they can bring the supplier element into the process.

Develop "Design Change Friendly" Supplier Quote Cost Breakdown Worksheets

Competitive bidding typically drives lower upfront supplier prices when the sourcing carrot is dangled in front of them, so many suppliers try to "make back their money" on design changes after they have been locked. And, at least in the auto industry, post-sourcing design changes during the product development process and even after mass production can be a huge cost driver. Many companies don't have either the time or a very good method of analyzing design change costs.

The gist of this cost savings idea is to provide an example of a worksheet that easily enables analysis of design change costs. While the worksheet I provided (see Appendix) is an example to illustrate the benefit is of my own creation, Honda used something along these lines, and I remember having great success with it there.

Here's how to decipher the fictional (but based on factual previous experiences) story found in the Excel spreadsheet:

The spreadsheet worksheet named "Typical Supplier Quote Cost Breakdown Worksheet" shows a commonly used quote breakdown worksheet for a part that has undergone a design change from a Revision Level 1 to a Revision Level 2. The supplier was already sourced the business at $1.98 through a competitive bidding process done at the Revision Level 1 design. You can see the selling price of the part after the design change to Revision Level 2 jumped to $2.30. Even though the supplier provided a cost breakdown of the $2.30 price, how can we quickly tell whether this is a good number? The supplier has been sourced, so we can't use another round of time-consuming competitive bidding to verify cost competitiveness. The answer would be to require the supplier to provide their quote breakdown in a format like the ones found on the two spreadsheet worksheets named "Recommended Supplier Quote Cost Breakdown Worksheet."

This proposed new and improved quote breakdown requires the supplier to perform a clear cost walk from the old design to the new design. It leaves little room for suppliers to hide fat in their design change costs, since everything that has changed is clearly indicated. This enables a quick review of what happened in the change and can spark quick questions like those shown on the 1st of the two recommended worksheets. Once the supplier is challenged by these questions to justify their costs, positive results thru a re-quote usually occur, like the results shown on the 2nd of the two recommended worksheets. It causes the design change costs to easily be resolved in a fact-based manner, which should provide a fair solution to both the customer and supplier. And, being that there is now less opportunity to hide fat in their costs, the suppliers will be less likely to attempt to do so on future changes.

This type of breakdown sheet can also be used to analyze new model part costing as well. I recall using this type of methodology on the new model 1998 Honda Accord. During the early product development stages and before sourcing the 1998 Accord Lighting parts, we asked suppliers to develop design ideas to take (I believe) 30% out of the price of the current parts. The goal was to help understand the design competitiveness of the suppliers to assist in the supplier selection process. We required the use of these types of sheets for their responses so we could easily see both the design and cost walk between the current part and their new model proposal. And, as you probably know, there is usually cost creep between the "Job Last" price of a part phasing out of production, and the "Job 1st" price of the new model design replacing it. This type of spreadsheet can help control that type of cost creep.

The nice thing about this breakdown worksheet is that it can be developed and up and running in a matter of hours. It takes virtually no investment, yet the payback can be huge.

One thing came to mind similar to the type of cost breakdown spreadsheets we used at Honda. Back there, the main commodity that I used this type of spreadsheet on was Lighting parts (Headlamps, Tail lamps, etc.). These parts are fairly complicated with a lot of components, so they required lots of line items on the spreadsheet. This being the case, I even seem to remember the supplier quoting using 11" x 17" paper to be able to fit it all in legibly! It worked, though, and it was nice having it all laid out on one piece of paper. (As an aside, that was another interesting thing at Honda. Most everything was done on one piece of paper. For instance, if we had a sourcing strategy to review with management, we made sure our analyses all fit on one sheet. That's another whole story though . . .)

* * *

It grew like Topsy.

Supplier costs. When an end user maps the supplier network—the Bill of Material structure—on a complex product, such an auto, or a cell phone, they will find the network branching out to too many levels to track. Sometimes a second or third tier supplier is subcontracting work that might be better done in-house. Sometimes the outsourced process is very special and must remain with the specialty supplier, and sometimes it can be moved back in-house to reduce product complexity and cost. The only way this consolidation can be highlighted is by doing a Bill of Material analysis diagram that covers the sources of all components and raw materials. The savings opportunity here is similar to the savings originally pitched for subcontracting, from 10-20 % generally. But the savings are now generated by factors not limited to reduced labor costs—things like handling and quality.

* * *

Michael Marks, CEO Flextronics

The industry is struggling a bit. We're all struggling to find a place in the big three, and there may be some consolidation, and markets for technology are not that great. As a company we are running $17B , next year we'll do $20B. We're spending a lot on the design side, building up and providing more design capability to customers, trying to execute. We're doing a really good job of managing cash flow metrics in execution mode. In general our customers have more respect for us now because we are getting big, and we have some power in the supply chain. The industry has matured. Solectron is $12B, Sanmina $10, Jabil 6 or 7. If you aren't $5B, you don't get to play. We are a survivor with good cash flow.

Things to do to save money—

For small and medium sized companies, today there are

174

things that we do. I think a lot of big companies need to be more aggressive, but there is so much hierarchy. What would I do if I were running a big OEM? There'd be a lot less people working there, because as they get bigger, they get more layers. For instance, there are giant HR departments, and marketing. But small companies don't do all that stuff. That's why they create jobs and make decisions quicker. All companies, my own included, need to work really hard to whittle down to five people where there used to be 30-40. It's not outsourcing, but eliminating the layers. We just don't have it. We went from 30 to five by combining, eliminating corporate headquarters. Every time we do an acquisition, we take out administrative overhead,

Another approach is the great use of outsiders, particularly with India, China, Eastern Europe. It's critical to put certain functions where they can be most cost effective, like splitting up and moving manufacturing or software design. For R & D, it's more complicated, and it depends on the kind of design.

We have very significant corporate procurement. We used to do procurement in the regions. Now we are buying through a big group in Asia, one in Colorado. We have very big contracts globally. Procurement is where we live and die now, dealing with relatively low margins in a high spend on materials.

* * *

Bill Michels, CEO
ADR North America
Ann Arbor, Michigan
bill.michels@adrna.com

It doesn't matter whether you are huge or small, this is area that is incremental profit. Purchasing is a key area, and the first thing we do in a client company is we make sure we separate the transactional purchasing from core purchasing, because if somebody is worried about chasing a truck or getting material to a line or plant, they can't really focus on cost improvement. By removing the day to day activity, Buyers are able to focus on cost improvement without distraction.

Example: We are working with a food company that uses plastic bags. We're looking at what all the product lines are using—different thicknesses, some were way too thick, 1 mil to 3 mil. When we realized there were really only 3-4 different thicknesses that would get the optimal amount of bag for packaging, that we could eliminate resin— about 10%— we went to one or two thicknesses, with one across most of the product line.

In one of the cases, we took 400M out of 1B spend— 40%— that was a complete transformation in a pharmaceutical company. We got the right alignment in the area of R & D by matching the tech capability of the buyer with the R & D dept. When you do focus on purchasing, you get the language, savings.

The other thing that is most important when using purchasing teams, is that they need cost management skills. They have to understand the cost drivers, or they will have no idea where to look at the item for reduction. We use purchase price cost analysis. We say the buyers can't really buy unless they can break up the cost into labor and material, overhead and profit. Take the example of a purchasing person that weighed up the cost of a can and found it was 50% less than they were quoted. Where it is high labor, they may go to a low cost country sourcing, or automated factory, but you really have to understand how is overhead allocated.

When visiting a plastic molding facility the overhead allocation was questioned. The company responded you are 21% of our sales and 21% of our overhead. They had 50 machines and we were only using 2 machine centers, but if the buyer doesn't know to ask that question, they won't see that opportunity.

You also have to segment the expenditure in a Portfolio Analysis to understand where the quick opportunities are. Is it a category where many suppliers are competing and values are high?

* * *

Life cycle management used to be a challenge for engineers and buyers, but as life cycles shrink to commodity timeframes— for cell phones it's less than six months— the investment in new products becomes more difficult to manage. It's not just a matter of having good suppliers involved from day one. It takes good life cycle management software to track the changes and optimize costs while obsolescence is minimized. YOU CAN ONLY DO WITH THIS SOFTWARE, not Excel spreadsheets.

* * *

cindyjimmerson@msn.com
President, Lean Healthcare West
(406)239-2467

My clinical background is nurse trainer/manager in emergency care and development of trauma systems, and I now help hospitals save money by being leaner. Believe me, there is a ton of opportunity there! What we do is apply the principles of the Toyota Production system to healthcare, and by fixing processes, we reduce waste (dollars and time), errors and make people like their jobs better as we fix system issues that have long frustrated the people delivering care. We look at work processes, maybe in the kitchen, the ICU, wherever, then we go in and do what lean folks do for manufacturing.

We use lean tools to look at the work and to find out why it is not consistent and reliable. We do problem solving using a Toyota tool that demonstrates the potential savings of dollars and time for that specific activity. Overall it takes up to five years in an organization for all the small improvements to accumulate to get the savings that administrators are after. We help the staff work on a million specific things in the course of their work and measure activity by activity what improvement is made.

We have used standard work to develop trauma programs such as life flight. Initially It was hard work, frustrating, because it's a broken system. It's difficult to try to fix processes in healthcare because there is 60 percent waste and administrators are still looking for the big bang that will fix things all at once. The system is going broke and can't meet baby boomer retirement demands. One solution is applying lean principles. Take the waste out, improve the service and make healthcare workers like their jobs more and make that part of everyday work, not a special "project."

* * *

Figure out what your spend is and where. You may have to call in some temps or an intern, but if you don't know what it is, you won't ever get your arms around the savings. Plus, when your team has the spend number, they can negotiate from an informed position. The only way to understand what the true cost of an item should be — sometimes the Japanese call this the "should cost"— is to break it down into all its true components: labor and materials mainly, but also machines used to process should be factored in, with packaging and transport. This is not the price that might be negotiated between a supplier and customer, but it is a calculated price rolled up from all the elements that contribute to cost.

One cost cutting team hit ten percent by studying all the items in their plastics commodity spend. Resin is a raw material with a very dynamic market price structure, and leverage—consolidating the spend—helps open the ears of the big resin suppliers.

Some end users let their molding suppliers deal with the resin suppliers, but this won't get you the price savings, because the spend needs to be big enough for them to pay attention. Generally the molders are happy to let their end customer negotiate prices for what they need, and they watch ongoing ship quantity triggers. Basically what you are doing is taking the purchasing job away from the subcontractors. It's a change, but it will save you money.

* * *

Dave Curry
Lasalle, Michigan
dacurry@charter.net

WHERE PURCHASING CAN LOOK FOR COST SAVINGS:

1. Outsource tactical activities like IT, indirect purchasing, logistics, security, payroll and janitorial

2. Re-negotiate payment terms.

This is something that you can usually get significant savings on, if you're either paying a net or 1 or 2 percent terms, negotiate something better. If you are going from 1 percent, go to 2 percent so you will have doubled your savings.

Things you can negotiate with suppliers, depending on their situation and status. We did a purchase order draft (POD) for a lot of the small, repetitive items that we bought. We would send a blank check along with the purchase order and the supplier would fill it out for the amount, which would have a limit like $50K. That eliminated the invoicing and allowed us to negotiate even better terms from them on costs because they were getting paid up front. You could probably do the same thing paperless, with EFT.

3. Reverse auctions for commodity type items

4. Consortium purchasing for the whole supply chain

There are two forms of this activity; the first is with small and medium size companies, where the companies add their volumes to leverage cost, and the second one is where you go in to the big co, take advantage of the leverage they already have and pass it on to their supply chain.

5. Raw material purchasing program

Honda did this, for several reasons, cost not the only one. They offered suppliers a chance to get their raw materials through Honda, the same thing as group purchasing activity—steel, for example. All Honda's stamping suppliers have the opportunity to buy their steel from Honda at a guaranteed price. Where Honda makes out is now their suppliers are buying at a firm price, a discount level they couldn't get on their own. Also, Honda has huge savings from the quality aspect, because now Honda is basically in control of the quality, and the supply base doesn't have to get involved with the quality, and they are able to save in that area, so they can give Honda better overall costs.

6. Supplier productivity improvement

Design for manufacturability, throughout the supply chain. Example of '98 Accord, took 26 percent cost out, mostly with design for manufacturability, Phase II BP, with the supply base.

7. Supplier Survey

Hard to put a number on it . Most customers are doing things that cost their suppliers money, and most times suppliers are reluctant to say anything, so they pass on those customer costs to them in the long run. If you do the survey, ask what are we doing that costs you money, because it can get passed on in higher prices.

8. Supplier incentives for V/E & V/A ideas

Some of these are closely related to the one on design for manufacturability— not always in the design but it's the same principle.

9. Suggestion system that extends to suppliers

Mentioned in *Powered by Honda* book, extending out to suppliers through the supply chain, getting them hyped about it. When Honda went from about 1,000 supplier people working on improvements to 10,000, that's 10,000 people, each working to make Honda product better. That's a powerful force, so suggestion system is real benefit.

10. Eliminate all unneeded inventory

11. P-cards or other streamlined systems purchasing. This has been around for quite a while. Average cost of a PO is $75-300. If you can eliminate that and eliminate invoicing and check writing, you get definite savings by giving people a purchasing card with a limit. For example, for maintenance people, you negotiate with a supplier for bearings and power transmissions. Pay for it with procurement card, and you are going to give them a list of authorized people. You get the credit cards, give them to the maintenance people. When they need a bearing, they go get it, no paperwork, and all the banks all have systems where you get your reports itemized, showing the credit card number, who did, what was purchased—the checks and balances are there. All the tactical stuff goes out of purchasing, but you still have control.

12. Purchase vs. lease analysis

There is software to do it, but lots of people don't take the time, even though there can be significant savings. When it comes to capitalizing, it depends on different tax laws, etc., programmed into the software.

13. Early warning system for supplier problems

14. Consignment purchase agreements

You can save money because you don't pay for a thing until you use the parts; storage is negotiable. Typically the customer provides the storage, but not paid for parts until pulled out of the inventory.

15. Right sizing of procurement

16. Recycle and sell trash, eliminate disposal cost

17. Make sure Purchasing is responsible for all of the spend

18. Right-size number of suppliers

19. Government grants for training

20. Having the right suppliers

21. Efficient monitoring of supplier performance numbers, so areas in need of attention are quickly identified

22. Line-side JIT delivery of OEM parts

23. Accurate target costing

24. Timely sale of obsolete parts and materials

With computer systems it's really easy. Every month you get printout of items that haven't moved in a year. Then you evaluate those items. If you return them annually, they are worth something, but if you wait five years they are probably not worth anything. Do it annually for larger percentage of money back.

25. The use of returnable containers

This goes beyond the containers. We're still seeing people use wooden pallets and corrugated boxes where they should be using returnable containers and returnable pallets. Who can help you figure that out? Anybody that sells the product. If you are using a lot of wooden pallets, contact a plastic pallet maker, have them come in and do the work, see what we are doing, see the numbers used and give cost comparison. Challenge the supplier. They aren't there just to sell you things, they are there to improve things. They need access to the floor—give them a badge, give them a tour, a desk. Get them out there and familiar with the people on the floor, and challenge them. When I was in charge of MRO, we had requirements for all primary suppliers to turn in a certain number of suggestions per year to improve. They are the experts! For lighting, for example, the cost of replacing lightbulbs is more than the cost of the lightbulb itself, so replace whole sections at a time, whether it's on or off, once you figure out what the average life is. Don't do 2 or 3 at a time; it's cheaper to throw them all away all at once than to nickel and dime it.

26. Use the most advantageous accounting for capitalized items

27. Supplier indemnification

If there is a lawsuit stemming from an accident and somebody sues the company and whomever made the parts, usually the supplier that made parts is smaller, so the strategy is to go after the deep pockets. The attorney for injured party would go to the supplier and get a real easy settlement with them, and because they got a settlement, they could use it in court to go after the big company. So tell suppliers they don't have to carry indemnification insurance, we will cover you and it is our sole responsibility to handle any litigation. They don't get held up, they control the payout, and the company handles the whole thing. It's a big advantage. The suppliers don't have to carry that insurance because the company carries it in their name, which saves on legal costs, settlement fees, and also it saves suppliers money.

28. Use phone cards for travel, instead of hotel long distance rates, where a 10- minute call costs $25.

29. Strong PPA - Potential Problem Analysis

* * *

Samples cost money

A buyer told me this story. He used to work doing engineering trials. For carpeting and headliners, the designers would want a different type of carpeting for engineering samples. His department would order the materials— sometimes it would take a whole 100-foot roll—make the samples and ship them out as samples, then cut and mail an invoice and wait for a response. Obviously, with parts in hand, the invoice would get lost, and it would turn into a writeoff.

His team process flowed it, and it looked like a spider web! The requests came through different departments. So they streamlined the process, 40 blocks to a dozen. They inserted stop gates, "do not proceed until this happens." What had been an ordinary expense totaling about $50,000 per year dropped to almost zero. No parts were ordered for raw material until the PO was received by the system and the item was shipped; the system created an invoice at the same time. The old way shipped the invoice to Joe the engineer, and he was expected to put it in the system. The new process allowed the team to show a profit on this line instead of a write-off!

* * *

Move the money faster.
When Accounts Payable reports in to Procurement, or they both report to the CFO, it's easier to accelerate a quote to cash. You might not be able to bill as built, like Dell, but you can sure shorten the time between when an order ships and the cash hits the bank. If Accounts Payable doesn't report to Procurement, try pulling together a Money Hungry Team to map the process and look for holes.

* * *

The Japanese use an approach to reviewing the numbers that they call Jikon. We call it open book accounting. Basically the idea is to share cost information about components in such a way that both parties can begin to develop real in-depth expertise about what it takes to produce a part correctly and efficiently. The idea is that a supplier's margins are protected in this type of discussion, so the open book approach works well in many situations. We like to use open book on a couple of our commodities where we have long standing relationships with certain suppliers. With others we would not attempt it.

* * *

Glenn Luckinbill
President & CEO
Optimal Supply
Glenn@optimalsupply.com

Price Leveling (Internal Benchmarking)

At a large integrated oil and gas company, simply reviewing all existing contracts for a given commodity resulted in identification of huge opportunities. For example, the company had six separate contracts with a solvent management company. The prices for like items varied by nearly 50%. Oddly enough, the best pricing was realized by one of the smallest business units with the smallest demand for the service. Simply consolidating the six contracts into a single contract at the lowest price resulted in average savings of 18%.

Benchmarking (External)

Many companies participate in benchmarking activities within their industry or with non-competitors. A number of small benchmarking companies focus on reviewing pricing and identifying opportunities to reduce third party pricing. You can also study your competitors' product or service to see what they might be doing differently (i.e., better). Participate in industry-type activities or benchmark with non-competitors to compare pricing.

Outsource Procurement

Many companies do not do procurement well. Typically they have two choices if they want to improve return on third party spend: 1) They can go through the painstaking process of changing the organization, processes, systems or 2) They can replace some or all of the internal organization, systems and processes with a third party procurement company. Companies such as IBM, Accenture, and Optimal Supply have developed these offerings and are delivering extraordinary savings to their clients who outsource the function.

Aggregation

Example 1: GM used to operate as five separate car companies, with a separate purchasing organization set up for each company. GM consolidated the purchasing function into a single Worldwide Purchasing (WWP) Organization. Source of Value was reduced, head count requirement and increased negotiating power/leverage.

Example 2: A large appliance manufacturer had 9 assembly plants and each plant had its own purchasing department responsible for procurement. In six months, the company created a central purchasing function and took over $20 million out of their $200M spend.

Example 3: At a large integrated oil and gas company, prior to 2003, each company-owned retail store (4,000 of them) contracted for waste disposal services independently. By going to market with a bid for all 4,000 stores, the company was able to reduce average waste disposal costs by over 25%.

Global Sourcing/Low Cost Country Sourcing

Example 1: One Detroit automaker included the development of global networks for each commodity. As a result, their North American buyers work together with buyers in Europe and Asia to identify and develop qualified suppliers in Eastern Europe and Asia. On leaf springs for pickup trucks, the company saved over 30% by buying from a supplier in India versus the incumbent North American suppliers.

Example 2: A large integrated oil and gas company purchased heat exchangers from local fabricators. The company ran a global reverse auction and identified qualified Korean fabricators that saved almost 50% net of logistics. There was huge reluctance to use Korean suppliers at first, but eventually the Procurement and Finance organizations wielded enough influence to convince Operations and Maintenance to source offshore and save the money. Now most heat exchangers come from two fabricators in Korea.

Example 3: Pipe prices for the automatic fire protection Industry doubled in the first half of 2003, and on a number of occasions lead time on pipe exceeded 16 weeks. Optimal Fire Protection was at risk of delaying major construction projects, but by looking offshore (to India) was able to find pipe and paid 30% less than domestic prices, net of logistics and import taxes.

Example 4: Offshore engineering is roughly half the cost

of onshore engineering. Optimal EPC, LLC is working with an engineering company in India and is realizing a 60% savings versus domestic engineering. EPC companies such as Fluor, KBR and Jacobs have begun to utilize offshore drafting and engineering.

Long-term Commitments

In some industries, such as automotive, "life of part" contracts have become standard. However, in many industries, purchasing decisions are made annually or on a project by project basis. One of the things suppliers value is long term commitment in the form of percent of business commitments or even better, take-or-pay contracts. In many cases, suppliers will extend significant discounts if you are willing to make a long-term commitment. The Asian automotive companies receive favorable pricing not only because of the detailed costing work done by buyers, but also because the supplier can count on retaining the business in the future as the Asian manufacturers are committed to working together over the long term to eliminate waste.

In a number of bids, we have asked suppliers to identify what incremental discount they would extend in exchange for a longer term contract (7-10 years). The number they come back with is often around 10%. This was the case with industrial cleaning contracts at a large integrated oil and gas company. Again, there are risks associated with this, including market price fluctuations. This can be mitigated with indexing, periodic price adjustments and other derivatives such as price ceilings, price floors, etc.

Take back the supply chain

As Motorola has done, a number of companies have taken back the supply chain. In the early 1990s, automotive parts were often purchased on an FOB delivered basis. In the second half of the decade, the big three automotive companies took control of inbound logistics and set up third party logistics providers who successfully established milk-run collections and eliminated billions of dollars of inventory on hand. In 1997, GM extended this philosophy to international shipments and significantly reduced the cost of importing parts from low-cost country sources.

Buying consortia

Not necessarily a quick hit, but can be a huge opportunity to aggregate spend across multiple companies. A number of consortia were started and failed in the dot com bubble. (e.g., Trade Ranger for oil and gas industry). However, a number still exist and it may be possible to join them. (I'm not up to speed on the current status of these consortia in other industries).

American Express has established "Open", a program for small businesses. The program offers discounts on office supplies, travel and restaurants.

In 2000, several large steel consumers looked at developing a steel buying consortium. This never materialized due to the perceived complexity and perceived cost to implement. However, after steel prices doubled last year, each probably wishes it had moved forward with the consortium. Other examples of industry consortia certainly exist.

Other generic ideas:

Enterprise sourcing systems

Reverse auctioning

Systems rationalization/standardization

Replace traditional buyers (i.e., paper pushers) with strategists.

Remove spending authority from operations and give it to procurement.

Simplify purchase to pay process.

Pay your suppliers on time. (You'll get better pricing in the future.)

Organize your teams in terms of spend categories (not regions).

Sourcing tables—Create a formal approval process with clear DOA .

* * *

One company used eBay to sell $30,000 of unused equipment—a printing press, one old injection-mold machine, carts and racks. Found money. They also bartered equipment with a local bartering company, which freed up space and earned points for the exchange—which they could use for baseball tickets, etc.

* * *

Dave Nelson,
Vice President, Global Supply Management
Delphi Corporation, former head of purchasing
at John Deere and Honda of America

To save money on indirect and direct materials, divide purchasing spend into direct and indirect. There are big savings in both areas.

On indirect:

One approach is a team—not of the top people,VPs or higher, but the real people, good high level managers and above—to look at the scope of your indirect spend. Have the team work on establishing how much indirect you buy— the major elements, the suppliers and the countries. The group can then make a recommendation to management as to how to blitz indirect and save a ton. This method can be used well with IT, for example, as well as MRO in the factories.

The idea is to unleash the creativity of a team. Don't give them much direction, just say, "We need savings, we want to improve profit. Look at the indirect spend, and do whatever you need to do to research it. You're trying to get as many ideas as you can." Be sure to include non-purchasing people—packaging might be a key area, or logistics/transportation—and let them go to work. The team will come back with many recommendations, some of them crazy, but that's okay. It's brainstorming at a high level, and management can decide if they want to take any of the recommendations that would constitute policy decisions, such as instead of providing corporate cars, give a stipend instead. If your company has never done this before, it's virgin territory. Just be sure to dollarize the ideas at the beginning.

Here's another MRO example—lightbulbs! Just about every global company buys huge numbers of lightbulbs all over the world, all locally from different suppliers. Most of them spend millions on lightbulbs with no contracts whatsoever. So your savings would be 30-40%, mainly because everybody buys locally . Even if you searched and found the lowest price in every region, it would be at least 30% savings.

Direct:

The same principles apply for direct materials that apply to Indirect. Form a high level team to go after direct materials costs. The team has to include engineers because they are going to study products, particularly in :

1. standardization of specifications
2. Value Analysis, Value Engineering.

Here are examples of savings ideas:

One team looked at items used locally, like cable ties, and decided they could get by with five different types instead of hundreds.

Plastics! Most companies have too many specifications for plastics. Expect your team to reduce the number of different types of plastics to fewer than 20 to save money.

Here's another opportunity area—transportation and logistics. Not even 2% of all companies optimize this area, and it's huge. I have seen companies project saving 20% like falling of a log. Another huge area is packaging, because most decentralized companies normally do not buy packaging centrally with a commodity team. They let the individual plant order whatever it wants, at a 20-30-40% premium. Same thing for office supplies.

Fasteners, another specification and standardization opportunity. One team found five fasteners that were exactly the same, with five different part numbers and five engineering specs, at 22 different locations! Plus they discovered they had 4,026 fasteners when they could get by with 500—more savings!

Supplier Suggestions:

I have seen a company that created a web-based supplier suggestion system that collected hundreds of good ideas, but because nobody owned it, it needed attention. There were 600 ideas that totaled millions of dollars, but it took a small group of professionals working full-time to process every one of them. For each moneysaving idea, the approach is to share cost savings with the supplier.

* * *

Supplier Suggestion systems are one of the best ways to find savings opportunities. Be clear from the beginning how proposed savings will be shared, and track and research suggestions at least weekly. Don't let them accumulate unacknowledged, because the system will lose credibility.

* * *

I attended a conference in Detroit last winter. The audience was filled with suppliers and C-level executives. The interactive panel included representatives from large OEs, and two from large suppliers. Each panelist delivered a ten minute slide talk and then the Q & A began.

Someone asked a panelist that since he had seen both sides of the fence, the American and the transplant way, if he could describe the real difference between the way the Japanese work with suppliers, and the way American companies do it. He hesitated, and responded that it was a little dangerous for him to truthfully answer that question, because he said the Big Three would kick his ass if he could answer the way he really felt in his heart. Heads nodded recognition as he struggled to respond.

Suddenly one of the other panelists jumped in. He told an apocryphal story. He said that there are two types of companies. One is like a hunter that provides food for his family by killing his prey and bringing it home. The other type is like a farmer that nourishes his crops year after year. He waters and fertilizes the plants on schedule, rotates his crops annually, checks them nightly, and he keeps this garden weed-free. The farmer's livelihood depends on having good, rich soil prepared and ready year after year, so he practices all the best improvement techniques, such as contour farming, and plants new seed varieties. He protects his investment.

But the hunter lives a life of more uncertainly and risk. He's always looking for better hunting grounds, and usually they take him farther from home. He never really knows what he'll bring home for supper, and his family suffers for that. When the hunter gets old or injured, he can no longer hunt, and his family starves. But when the farmer gets old, he can still help in the garden as the rest of his family tends crops. Somehow, even during the winter, the farmer and his family survive.

* * *

Leroy Zimdars, Supply Chain Management Consultant
lzimdars@prodigy.net

Supply Chain Cost Savings Initiatives
Many companies today don't understand the power of a lean supply chain network. They are still operating with a large supply base. They have complex purchasing organizations with multiple purchasing locations, a bunch of suppliers, and no strategy to effectively manage their suppliers.

Example: A company that was a supplier to heavy construction equipment customers, a West Coast supplier of metal manufactured fabrications. Annual purchases were $40M, and $20M was in steel, so they had about $20M on other commodities. They bought fabrications, machining, paint and hardware. I went in there and looked at the commodities to find the big cost savings opportunities. I did the analysis and looked at where the bulk of money was being spent—in three locations, one in the Midwest, two on the East Coast—each facility operating independently. They said they had a corporate purchasing manager, but he had no control over the plants' purchasing activities. They bought 650 different machined part numbers through 44 suppliers. And that total dollar volume was $4M distributed among 44 different companies. We worked to consolidate machining suppliers in all three plants.

We looked at how to develop common suppliers for all plants while having unique ones based on geographic location and special services. We focused on the high volume parts. Over a three-month period of time the team determined that the 44 suppliers could be consolidated to five with savings of $750K. I provided them a process that they followed. Two people, both mfg engineers, did the work with purchasing support. We asked for the sharpest people who really knew cost structure and manufacturing processes.

Here is an overview of the process:

In the first phase, data collection, identify specifics; start with how many total suppliers, where they are located, number of parts they produce, plant's size, what processes available, what's the dollar spend.

Once you have that, interview stakeholders inside your company, to understand their opinion of the supplier's performance, design support, process technology, and their view of future plans that could phase out any of the machined parts. You want to be sure that their input be heard up front to help get their buy-in on the source decisions later.

For each current supplier, do a review of their overall performance and rate them. Consider quality, cost, timing, continuous improvement, lean manufacturing, financial viability, capacity, management style and geographic location. Match the scores with input from internal stakeholders, and decide on the companies that are the best fit and should be considered for a bid package.

Next, the bidding process. Submit the bid package/s including part drawings and samples. Require bidders to provide one unit price per part based on the total package of business (no quantity break pricing). This will allow you to have control of part pricing when you need to vary release quantities. Also, require full cost breakdown information on each part. This process should be completely electronic, including the cost breakdown form that you send them. Also, have them include data to confirm that they have the capacity to do this work.

When the completed packages come back from the suppliers, you should perform your analysis considering total cost of bid package including tooling costs, freight costs, etc. Once that's done, have a pre-award discussion with management—"Here's the plan, here is the impact of plan, do I have your support?"— and get them signed up.

There should be a project plan in place for each step of this process, but the real planning will go into the consolidation timing plan. It should be detailed and consider timing to build new tooling, PPAP and inventory build up from current suppliers.

When you get to the management review, you are coming in proud and ready – "Here is the amount of money we can save, and here's where we can save it. " Supplier consolidation will generate savings in the range of 20-30%, and you will have greatly reduced the complexity in managing your supply base.

That's one area that's good.

Another area is standardization. Standardize what you are buying. In steel, take a look at all the grades of material you buy, and ask why do we need to use the different grades of material. If you can use hot rolled steel in place of cold roll there is a 10-15% opportunity. Or if you can eliminate the need for special requirements like special sheet sizes or pickle and oil, you can save 5% or more. All these things start to add up. Look for opportunities like this on the design specification side.

Another example: a company that makes consumer lawn equipment. They were using an oil bottle (for crankcase) that had bottle specifications that made it a special according to the bottle manufacturer. I found a similar bottle that was a standard in the industry and used by other large customers. We were able to change to that bottle configuration and save the equipment manufacturer $1M per year in the cost of the oil bottle.

Another really good idea is to hire a sharp cost analyst. In most purchasing organizations, purchasing people aren't strong on cost analysis. A cost analyst can evaluate the spending in the larger dollar commodities and look for waste. It is important to have suppliers' cost breakdowns to help find those opportunities. When an experienced cost person starts asking questions about specific cost elements with suppliers, you generally find opportunities for continuous improvement that will drive out waste. You should easily get a 3:1 payback on the salary you are paying.

I have experience teaching suppliers lean manufacturing

practices. I hired a team of five continuous improvement engineers who worked full time with suppliers to improve their costs through implementing lean manufacturing practices. They would conduct C.I. events that took about 4-6- weeks to implement and delivered great results—higher quality, faster cycle times, less scrap and waste and overall lower costs which passed through in reduced pricing to my company. Today, many customers are requiring 5% or more price reductions per year from suppliers. This is a cooperative way to help teach suppliers how to achieve these price reductions without attacking their margins.

* * *

Anthony S. Nieves, C.P.M.,CFPM
Senior Vice President, Supply Management
Hilton Hotels Corporation World Headquarters,
anthony_nieves@hilton.com

WE WANT TO HEAR FROM YOU!
Tell us what we're doing well, and maybe not so well.
In our efforts to continually improve our service, Supply Management wants to hear from you. Simply click on this e-mail link (SM_Feedback@hilton.com) and send us your feedback, comments, and/or questions about our team members, products, services, suppliers, or anything else related to supply management. If a response is required, someone will contact you shortly. Thank you.
Product Rationalization – Analyzing your products can reduce your spend immediately. Product Rationalization is a comprehensive review of product specifications, a determination of how the product is utilized, and a review of alternative products. The goal is to identify potential cost savings opportunities without sacrificing product quality; benefits include: Increased quality levels, lower product cost, Increased productivity, improved overall standards and product knowledge, improved departmental relationships and communication, improved supplier relationship and communication.
Contract Compliance. Audit your contracts – It may seem simple, but if you are not actively auditing your contracts, the

potential for being overcharged is greatly increased. Set up an audit team to analyze products or services that were previous purchased for contract compliance.

Contracted Services. All companies have trash, but not all companies have contracts for trash removal. If you're not careful, you could be paying a lot more for service than necessary and you could be locked into an agreement that is not easily dissolved. One of the tactics a waste disposal company uses to retain a hotel's business is to add in a self – renewal clause. This clause renews the contract automatically with a short grace period or has specific cancellation terms that allow the contract to renew automatically if they are not followed. Analyze your current contracts and consolidate when necessary. Cell Phone Usage is another example - Company paid cell phone plans can be reduced for a quick savings. We have discovered that it is most likely that companies are being overcharged on their service plans for company paid cell phones. For example – some of the individuals might not need all the offered features such as call waiting, call forwarding, etc. Sometimes the minute plans are excessive for the usage of the individual. Does the individual consistently go under the minute plan which might need to be reduced? Are some of the individuals going over their minutes, which can lead to extra charges? Company employees do not typically analyze their own cell phone plans to optimize the efficiency. Your service provider can provide a breakdown of the service provided and also make recommendations. It is our recommendation to have an individual analyze all of the cell phone service plans to reduce costs.

Identify areas of non-traditional supply management involvement in corporate expenses like: Legal Counsel, Information Technology, Marketing, Advertising, Travel, Accounting/Audit firms, Insurance, Medical Insurance, Relocation, Temporary Workforce, Consultants, etc.

Measure compliance to programs (participation benchmark) and hold end users accountable.

Take a two pronged approach where feasible (negotiate the program directly with the manufacturer and then with the distributor)

Become a stockless distributor or merchant of record and develop programs directly with the manufacturer.

Handle the logistics and transportation directly with the freight companies rather than relying on the supplier to negotiate the best deal on your behalf.

Look for consolidation opportunities

* * *

Theresa Metty
Chair-Board of Directors; Institute for Supply Management
former CPO Motorola

Reduce complexity

Implement a formal program in partnership with engineering and product management that defines specific technology road maps for all key components and materials. By using formal check-points and integrated product design systems, you can restrict the ability of anyone to deviate from the agreed-upon road maps. By defining these road maps, you systematically reduce the natural tendency toward part number proliferation which, left unchecked, creates complexity that severely impacts Procurement's ability to effectively leverage purchases. It's a huge opportunity for big and small companies! In the cell phone business, batteries and displays are big complexity generators; in printers, it's cartridges and resins. By limiting the amount of complexity within any given category of spend, a company can easily lower component and material costs by 15-25%.

* * *

Blog Summary, MRO

Brad Holcomb
Vice President and
Chief Procurement Officer
Waste Management, Houston
BHolcomb@wm.com

1. Create a top-down and bottom-up culture of cost reduction. Get angry at wasteful spending. Have contests. Challenge each other across all divisions and departments to reduce costs by ten percent. Invite a resource ("detective") from a different department into your department to help identify cost reduction opportunities. Do the same everywhere. Set ten percent as a specific performance target, and measure performance against those targets every month. Post results in a very visible way for all to see. Make this objective part of the performance appraisal process at every level in the organization.

2. For categories such as office supplies and MRO, find suppliers that will develop specific "approved items" catalogs for your company. Select as many "generic" items as you can possibly stand—like "sticky notes" and pens/pencils/ tablets and recycled toner cartridges—and negotiate special pricing on those items. Measure and post compliance against those "approved items" and make the results visible.

It's like working with a Grainger—they can sit down with you and go down through things you buy—we don't need 300 flavors of gloves, we only need 20. If we can pour all our volume into those 20, then Grainger can go back, negotiate better pricing, put only 20 in the catalog, or they are starred as pre-approved items.

Then measure the organization as to how well they are aligning vs. one-offs (maverick buying). Better yet, don't let maverick buying happen!

We do the same thing with Staples' special on-line catalog. One hundred percent of office supplies are bought on-line through an Internet portal, and within that we have specifically put in the generic post-it notes, the remanufactured toner cartridges and the types of pencils and pads that we want. Fifty percent of the cost of some branded products can be saved. On office supplies, totaling $6-7M per year, we saved at least 30 percent.

3. Develop a scorecard mechanism that holds all divisions and groups accountable for compliance against all negotiated contracts. If the contracts aren't good enough, fix them as opposed to working around them. In other words, wage war on "maverick spending." It should not be tolerated. Measure and post overall compliance across the company.

At Waste Management, we have perfected it. We had a war on maverick spending going on for three years. We have 1,200 sites, 1,200 districts. A hauling company might have five trucks or 200, and they all buy stuff and roll up to regional offices, but we look, through Peoplesoft, and we can see every nickel of spend – every nickel spent, what suppliers use and how much, whether they are approved or non-approved suppliers. We track the ratio of approved suppliers, called supplier partners, compared to total spend.

Compliance is so powerful. It starts with a directive from the head of our company, Dave Steiner. The scorecard covers a handful of dimensions that each site is measured against every month—safety, maintenance practices, procurement and customer service. We measure people through hard data, and we score them and we quartile them. We know who is the top quartile organization., and we give trophies at the annual leadership conference in Las Vegas. When the president gives the award, the message is get better or get out. There is no tolerance for mediocrity, and in this procurement area we have moved the marker from 75 percent compliance to our procurement contracts and approved suppliers, to 99.6 percent. Virtually everybody is totally on board with the approved suppliers.

The next piece is when everybody is on the program, if there are problems with it, like if somebody says, I understand Grainger is the approved supplier for this motor, but I found it for a lower price across the street. Then I say, okay, bring it to me, and I will get that price with Grainger. I'll work with them, partner with them to make it happen and to continuously improve. When problems occur, I am not going to jump ship and they won't jump ship.

The reason these deals are so good is that we develop them in a cross-functional fashion. If they are bad deals, no mandate would produce 99. 6 percent compliance. We measure compliance every month, and everybody can see what everyone is scored at.

In Atlanta, for example, we have two or three different sites—one better than another, they should help each other. They should have an informal buddy system. Built into their compensation, each person develops a PDS Plan (performance driven success plan), and that's a component of everyone's career evaluation, annual compensation and goals and evaluation. The guys in the cellar see the consequences around their job security through the lens of the scorecard—it's data driven, and we see true performance. This has been ongoing for three years. If there is no movement in a year, we do a diagnostic to see if there are legitimate reasons or not. For example, if Waste Management bought a small company and they all had bad trucks, we would not penalize on maintenance on the scorecard. But it turns out to be bad management, we will make change based on the scorecard. This, to me, at this level of discipline, is a best practice. It's what I call the magic, the internal scorecard.

4. BONUS. Involve procurement in the commercial work. Involve them from the very beginning, even at the conceptual stage. If any department or group is not confident that their procurement team can/should be involved at that early stage, you either have the wrong type of people in procurement or the wrong type of thinking in the customer groups! There is virtually no area of significant spend, from office suppliers to contract, legal or other pro-

fessional support, to benefits packages, to basic materials and nuts and bolts, that the right type of procurement talent cannot add significant value to. There should be no "sacred cows," and no spend whatsoever that is "off limits" to procurement. If your procurement department does not measure up to this challenge—fix it, and fix it now!

* * *

Rick Ankrum, C.P.M., A.P.P.
Purchasing Manager - National Purchasing
SYSCO Corporation, Houston, TX
Ankrum.Rick@corp.sysco.com

Reduce spend for MRO items by speeding up the ordering process by utilizing a requisitioner ordering system. Procurement analyzes the spend of a particular group of items, negotiates with suppliers for the best overall value and empowers the requsitioners to order when they need the goods. Procurement negotiates the pricing and terms, a team can assist in selecting the supplier, and the requisitioner decides when and how much to order. Now requisitions do not pile up in Purchasing. Requisitioners get the materials when they need them at the negotiated price. The supplier works with the requisitioner on specific requisition needs, and procurement manages the full relationship rather than getting bogged down in chasing orders. Information will be paramount in this scenario, so that procurement negotiates the right items for the right price for delivery in the right time frame. The team helps with end user acceptance (usually not a hard sell since they will be empowered).

* * *

Michael Gruis, C.P.M., A.P.P.
MRO Buyer
Tyco Safety Products
Marinette Operations
715/735-7411 x3216

There are simple opportunities in the utilities spend at every facility. Electricity, fuel, etc., provide fairly easy opportunities to bring more cash to your company's bottom line. We are beginning a project of replacing our old lighting system with a new, highly efficient lighting system that will have a ROI of less than 2 years on an investment of $100,000.

On natural gas, if you buy direct from your local utility, you always pay the "spot buy" or current market price. There are organizations out there that offer services to look ahead and forward buy on this commodity and lock in a more favorable price. Depending on market conditions, a company can save thousands of dollars on this as well. Organizations that practice "spot buying" in areas like this are playing catch up with their savvy competitors.

Utilities is a commodity that every MRO Buyer should take a look at for cost saving opportunities.

* * *

Jim Bergman, Supply Mangement Consultant
jimjbergman@att.net

1. Join consortiums for office supplies, MRO and travel. Based on my conversations with Staples, United, HP and a few others over the years, I am certain the supplier side of the equation is willing to extend at least ten percent reductions if there is an aggregated spend.

Let's use office supplies for the example. Our company, company X, has $50K in annual spend, and we get only a three percent discount. If we join a consortium with 20 other members in it, we have an aggregated spend of over $1 million. As a consortium, we will get a 15 percent discount. The consortium can be organized and operated by one of the members, but it always proves to be a fatal hassle. An external firm can organize it and run it for an administrative fee. The office supply supplier usually is willing to allow a forecast of spend during the first year or two, allowing the consortium to prove itself and establish a spend level. After that, the discount levels are adjusted accordingly, sometimes lowered. But at least some short term savings can be realized.

2. Make the next phone call to the phone company. All of the major voice and data providers are willing to cut deals, especially SBC. If the customer steps up to Term Commitments, there are discounts to be realized, plus the base rates are continuing to drop, but keeping a focus on those rates is essential. As long as they are on the phone, get a cell phone pooling arrangement. Overall cost reduction opportunities are significant (at least 20 percent). You have to review your comm bills every month, look for mistaken charges, long distance, etc., and then go to them.

Term Commitments allow the customer to look at their past few years of spend. Let's say it averages out to $1.5 million in voice and data charges per annum. Sign a three year, $3 million Term Commitment (not a $4.5 million Term Commitment) and the Telecom supplier will give you reduced rates.

What's a cell phone pooling arrangement? If you have a plan for 1,000 minutes/month at $100/month, and 1,000 employees have cell phone plans, you are paying at least $100,000/month for all those phones. In fact, you will be paying more, because some folks go over their 1,000 minute allotments and you are paying $120 or whatever due to the excess minutes. With a cell phone pooling arrangement, the 1,000,000 minutes can be bought as a lump sum package for less than $100,000. Some people will use less than 1,000 minutes. Some will use more than 1,000 minutes. As long as the group as a whole uses no more than 100,000 minutes during the month, there are no excess usage charges. The savings are twofold—greater leverage/volume discount and avoidance of usage overage fees.

3. Ask one of your customers who is a larger corporation whether they're planning on conducting an electronic reverse auction and, if they are willing, add your spend to their event as a separate lot. This is at least a ten percent opportunity.

When you say in a separate lot, do you mean the auction bidders/respondents will know that mr. smaller co. has a lot in the auction, or is that supposed to not be visible to the outside world, just to the guy who is letting you piggyback on his auction?

It is fine to add the additional lot in such a way that the bidders/respondents know who mr. smaller co. is. The respondents will need to know that before they respond, in order to factor in transportation/delivery costs, credit/payment risk, unique specifications, etc.

* * *

Blog Summary, IT

In a global company with hundreds of locations and lots of product variety, integration is a challenge. There is good growth and bad growth, and when we reward engineering for just developing new ideas, like the number of patents per year, but not for leveraging new designs off existing components, we create complexity, and that costs money Plus it's hard to change the rewards system. One company had 500 legacy systems which they chopped down to only five including sales planning, payables, asset management, indirect procurement, tools planning, supplier master file. It wasn't easy, but it made the numbers clearer and easier on suppliers.

They also developed an electronic bid and quote package, so that suppliers could log into a portal during the sourcing process. Once the sourcing decision is made, the trimmed down main system has all the back-up information.

* * *

Bryan D. Stolle, CEO/Chairman
Agile Software Corporation
www.agile.com

Our corporate slogan is "How products become profits."

A lot has changed in the way companies acquire and use IT, the size of the investment, and how much they are willing to invest until they are sure. We have 1,200 customers, and we are happy to have anyone talk with anyone. We pound the table and emphasize we want you to talk with our customers, to see what's really happened, ask about what's happened, ask how long did it really take, how much did it cost.

Two things are amazing about the whole process. First, it's amazing how little due diligence companies do, especially if they have spent sometimes three x or more their original estimate on other projects, had others go completely awry, or have ended up rev-locked because of excessive customization to make the application do what was originally promised. I continue to be surprised at how little the decision-making process has changed. Companies have radically changed how and how much they will pay for applications, but still haven't changed the selection process itself. We spend our fair share on enterprise software, and when we buy it, we go about it very differently than most companies.

Despite the malaise in enterprise software generally, we are seeing a new growth wave specific to Product Lifecycle Management (PLM). For instance, we are engaged in some very large implementations, but when we ask what else the customer is investing in or doing, it's a small, tight list. So how does this tie into the next big thing, three-five years out? In many ways, the world is just getting started with the Internet, and most of the focus has been to the customer-facing side. But really, the Internet can drive significant and fundamental shifts in how companies work together to deliver that offering to the customer. The Internet is still untapped in so many ways, but the reality is that almost anything that gets delivered to a customer is a product of many companies working together. There are huge inefficiencies, mistakes—wrong things shipped, product not as good as could have been, two suppliers didn't work together. It creates a whole new problem set because any time you expand the group of people working on something, you get friction. It's an old military axiom that the bigger and more complex an operation gets, the more confusion and uncertainty creeps in—friction. The system that is involved in delivering something to the customer has become so diversified and complex, and it is constantly changing.

On China—China is where Japan was in the '60s, only China is ten x bigger—their run at being the world's leader will go for a long time. But our political leadership is not thinking far enough ahead. The fact that you have to get elected every 2-4 years produces a shorter term focus. The electorate and the politicians have less time to think ahead. If it was up to me, I would require every politician to take a 2-week trip to

China—Shanghai or Beijing. Most politicians' image of China is as villages and towns of 2-3 story wooden structures, junks and sailing ships in a crowded third-world image. But the reality is that now, Shanghai is more modern than NYC. The first time anyone sees it, it blows their mind. Two weeks would do it, 1 week would do it, 2 days would do it to change their world view and understand the challenge the U.S. faces in this next century!

The more important point is that we truly live in a globalized economy. We've been talking about it for years, but *the reality is today any company, anywhere in the world, can get to your customers as well as you can*—because of the Internet and distribution. Anybody can figure out how to make it look right, and because of global logistics any competitor can deliver as easily as you can. We truly do live in global economy—even $100M/year companies, perhaps smaller, have to think globally and be global operations. We are $120M/ year, and we have development centers in San Jose; Suzhou, China; Bangalore, India; Montréal; and Karlsruhe, Germany. We are a global development organization and our products are used and supported globally.

On Dell logistics—They have done a very good job of being a global company and leveraging a global supply chain. They think about logistics in the design process, trying to meet design objectives, such as how to be cheaper and easier to ship and ship in a way that is not just a function of size and weight. It's also a function of asking, if we put product into smaller, lighter packaging, what happens, is it shock resistant? If you look at the cargo hold of a 747, probably 50-80 percent of volume is packaging, so that's a lot of money tied up in volume and packaging, keeping it safe as opposed to shipping it. We help people with that. If you have a collaborative system in place, it's easier to bring the logistics people on board to collaborate, to get them involved in the design process early on. For example, what kind of reductions can be made in the weight of a new notebook computer model? If you can figure out a way to reduce the packaging volume and weight but keep the product safe, you can ship twice as much product in the same volume.

* * *

Ken Marcia
Director of UTC Supplier Development
United Technologies
KENNETH.MARCIA@UTC.COM

A healthy supply base is essential to UTC's success. What does "healthy" mean? In part, it means suppliers who can keep their costs down so we can keep ours down. But that's not enough. Our suppliers must have the capabilities to not only minimize costs but also maximize quality and ensure timely delivery. And they have to be able to do so profitably, so that they remain healthy, sustainable and reliable businesses. That's why our Supply Management organization has been on a mission to share our knowledge and capabilities with our supply base.

This may sound costly, but the price of not pursuing this endeavor would be far greater.

Of course, the easy way out would be to simply demand lower prices from suppliers, which we must sometimes do. But this could put suppliers' profitability at risk. And far too many suppliers, particularly in the aerospace industry, are already at risk. If we lose a key supplier, we lose money and production time while we're getting a replacement up to speed.

So one of the things we focus on is trying to minimize risk in our supply base. The best way to minimize risk is to prevent it altogether. And the best way to do that is to act and manage in a predictive mode, not a historic mode—in other words, spot a potential risk before it becomes an actual risk and prevent it from occurring.

But even large companies do not have the resources to send enough people out into the field across their entire supply base to evaluate, prescribe and fix what's wrong to stomp out risk.

That's where Open Ratings software has been a powerful and helpful tool for us.

UTC was a kaizen pioneer but still only had resources to touch less than five percent of the supply chain. We weren't creating critical mass to improve fast enough. Today, with enhancements to the process, use of technology such as Open Ratings, and a significant increase in skilled lean experts called Operations Transformation Leaders (OTLs) whom we can send into the field, we can affect our supply base in a meaningful and positive way.

We use Open Ratings to evaluate suppliers' capabilities, monitor their performance, anticipate potential problems and take appropriate action. One factor we look at is whether financial performance problems could lead to a supplier going out of business The point is, we try to understand performance risk in the supply chain before it affects us. Armed with this information, we have on several occasions taken actions with suppliers to avoid business interruption—or worse, total shut down.

For example, Open Ratings has a Supplier Stability Indicator that alerts us to a supplier's increased risk of a cash liquidity problem. Then, if we think it makes sense to do so, we work with the supplier to improve its operations and cash flow so that we don't lose that supplier.

Case in point: A precision machining and assembly company that supplied one of our divisions with valve assemblies faced imminent performance problems. Unfortunately, the supplier's quality ratings were down, escapes were up, and the firm faced imminent bankruptcy. The costs and risks of sourcing these components elsewhere would have been prohibitive. Fortunately, with the help of Open Ratings, we knew all this before it came to a head. The supplier, to its credit, was willing to do whatever it would take to right the ship. We deployed some of our OTLs to the supplier's facilities. They conducted value stream mapping (VSM) events. We trained supplier personnel including top management in our quality toolkit and in lean techniques. The result: The supplier's quality ratings are now at or near 100 percent, lead time was reduced by 65 percent, and the firm earned a new contract from us that provides a hefty income stream while saving us more than $1M/year. A second case is where we received a financial alert from Open Ratings on a supplier that provides complex machined assemblies. This supplier was minority owned and strategic to one of our product lines. Supplier cash flow was negative, and once again we intervened with our

OTLs to remove waste and increase capacity. The supplier was able to ramp up production fourfold in a nine-week period of time. The end customer was more than satisfied and awarded a significant contract follow-on the next year.

These are not isolated incidents at UTC.
Open Ratings helps us determine where it makes the most sense to deploy our resources to assist our supply base. We can identify who is most at risk—or will be—and whether we should intervene. In short, Open Ratings helps us zero in on opportunities to take costs out and improve quality in a large and complex supply chain. I am not aware of any other supply management organization that has taken this predictive, proactive approach to the extent we have to improve our business globally by improving and strengthening our supply base.

* * *

Barbara Hoefle
Founder and VP of Product Planning
Serus Corporation
Mountain View, California
barbara@serus.com

What has been missing in the marketplace is software to take away the pain. Even after investing tens of millions of dollars on infrastructure and software, people are still in pain. They're using Excel, i2, Oracle, any panacea. There is a huge reality gap between analysts and marketing jargon, versus what people are experiencing and the real tools they are using.

Our software helps companies deal with the quote to cash cycle, but also it's about service oriented architecture.

In the area of Lean Manufacturing, we are helping minimize inventory across all contract manufacturing and suppliers—not just from the OEM's perspective, but from their customer's perspective as well. This isn't just one or two tiers of the supply chain, it is the entire Value Chain! This is to manufacturing what Wal-Mart is to "Point of Sale" global inventory collaboration!

We do optimization and what-if analysis, enabling users to change some parameters, see what happens with numbers, and then execute on those changes. The thing is, you don't want to take away the knowledge of your people through some "black box" approach. This is what drove Nike to blame software on their missed numbers! Our software gives the users the optimized solution set while leveraging their real-life knowledge, the stuff they take off-line and do in Excel simply because older software isn't flexible enough.

It's about managing by exceptions, using productivity enhancements because there is financial liability on inventory across the entire Value Chain, and it also goes into Sarbanes-Oxley compliance. Today companies need to track all changes and decisions across internal teams, as well as the collaboration push-pull that happens with your vendors, and be able to give a report to an auditor that clearly explains price changes, changes to negotiated rates, inventory liability, it goes on and on. Today this can equate to millions of dollars in "off-line" processing costs and staff resources, and it still isn't what auditors need!

People aren't just looking for smart software, they want a holistic solution that functions at the most advanced levels of technology that leverages internal knowledge cells while providing traceability and auditability across all tiers of the supply chain.

* * *

Stan Smith, CEO
Open Ratings
stanfordsmith@comcast.net
ssmith@openratings.com

I would say that many companies did overbuy in software, and with the downturn marking the end of the free spending days, they realized they had unused investments. As a percentage of internal assets, the investment was huge. In fact, I have talked with numerous companies that have an embarrassingly big number of software purchases—it's the hangover effect. I have also talked with a number of people, small players, who said that companies wanted the "big picture" solution, that despite knowing better they would take a $5-10M deal but they knew that in 2-3 years the customer would come back dissatisfied with the slow progress, the cost overruns etc. That has caused people to take a much harder look at what they will invest in when trying to cut spend.

So what should the software investment be today? My response to this scenario is: Only buy what you absolutely need as a product. Don't invest in something that causes you to do more work. Have vendors prove the actual value and impact of their solution. At Open Ratings we would offer a "Proof of Concept" approach that provided the customer with a study that analyzed a small portion of their supply base and gave them the results as a demonstration of our capabilities. At the very least they got value from the effort, even if they didn't proceed with the full solution, which by the way has never happened.

The solution is compelling enough that when they se the results they can easily justify moving forward. The reason we decided to have customers put forward cash is that they need buy-in from organization—it's earnest money, skin in the game—not a pilot, it's a snapshot. The cost is based on the size of the company, the number of suppliers—typical deals six-figure range.

We're talking about a business problem that is important enough to solve.

All major manufacturers are faced with significant supplier risk, and they are constantly asking their peers what they are doing to manage the risks. What happens next is the information gets out and people start benchmarking themselves against our customers. We have not spent any money on marketing. We're in aerospace, automotive, where we know the supply chain has been suffering, and where the average supplier is $5-50M per year in revenue. These suppliers can't afford the payment terms. They have gone through e-sourcing engagements, and they have very low margins. They are not efficiency experts, they make great products and they are probably great engineers. So when their best customer tells them to drop costs by 30 percent, they don't' know what to do, and maybe they end up losing money. Some of them don't even know they are losing money —there are no internal mechanisms to manage cash flow—they just feel good if everybody is employed.

So there has been upheaval. Quality has been hard to manage, the ability to deliver has become a great risk. The bigger company becomes more dependent on supply chain— and they can't see the risks before they show up.

We walk them through it and give them a chance to see the entire supply base, to identify the risks, as opposed to when an order doesn't show up on the shipping dock.

One area we use most is performance issues, which can be in some people's minds somewhat subjective, but when we look at financials, that's the one thing we use to determine a supplier's stability—and it's their bankruptcy score. It's a huge indicator. We rely on the fact that we can predict instability in suppliers, as our value depends on the accuracy of performance data.

Typically when we see changes in performance at a supplier, certain kinds, through our advanced analytics, there are a small number of situations that can show a company. is shutting down. We flag our customer to go check it out.

We go to the company and ask, have you lost any important suppliers in last 90 days, and with almost all of the ones in the markets we go after, we could have warned them prior to the event. It's the perfect global solution to the enormous global marketplace. This approach is intended to manage suppliers in the US, to get to know them, to build a long term level of trust, but if you move to a country with an unfamiliar culture—you can't socialize with them, for instance—the question becomes what to do when you have no infrastructure, when the business has moved offshore. We know we can help companies benchmark the current supply base against their supply base.

There's tons of data, and we have figured out about how to collect it, to aggregate and present it, to create knowledge. Every individual company. has large amounts of data. By pooling all this information, we can profile the customer site and see what information is relevant and what scale is relevant.

We see data on 30M transactions per month. Our focus is three verticals— aerospace and defense, automotive and heavy manufacturing. We define our target market today as companies with the highest cost of supplier switching, as opposed to knowing what's going on with this supply base. A supplier problem can be huge or little, but it's not something they can determine when and if it can happen.

We started in 1999 and went through the B2B bust. Our initial foray was to be the provider for those exchanges. We wanted to be a provider of information. So we became an enterprise software provider when B2B imploded. We had better, slower traction, and we had learned a lot working with earlier customers.

Now we are after early adopters that we are trying to move to early majority. There are early adopters, and then there are the ones looking for competitive advantage. We've taken a very analytical approach—high risk, high value if some number of these succeed.

UTC is a very consistent early adopter. Free Markets was one of very many —they have been a great company to have as an early adopter, and we learn together. The aerospace companies built the first of many new ideas—simulations, CAD/CAM - so they are one of most important, large early customers. If there was something they tried to build, that's a confirmation that there is enough of a business need, and we see they have done internal analytics, software, internal and external format. They've spent more money, but it hasn't given them the solution they needed. "Well," we said, "we can solve that problem for you." Aerospace has been forward thinkers, it's what's fun for us. We've gone from risk management into the supply chain improvement and development area. From the risk perspective, we have identified opportunities, we can categorize, and we have follow-on opportunities.

The result of this work has been that out of thousands of assessments, if there is one that a customer thinks there was significant departure from the results of assessment, instead of sending people on site to gather data, now they read the assessment, determine the big opportunity, send that one individual in to determine how to change the supplier's process. So we have a growing list of actual, exciting situations where we have companies that will talk openly.

We have a company, for instance, that was doing a sale—the customer had more demand than the supplier could handle, and so he was looking at new suppliers. But we found that the efficiency could be improved—from our data. As a result, the supplier's capacity increased, the customer sent more business and shut off certification of a new supplier. (It typically costs $0.5M to certify.) By concentrating more spend with the existing supplier, which became more efficient, their margins improved, and both shared in the benefits,

Customers are prioritizing. They want to look at the opportunities and relative benefits—to reduce risk or improve performance—where it is most important. They ask if they should single-source or if they spend a lot of money, can they reduce costs and improve quality. And what we have seen from customers is that there is a range from 6-10:1 increase in productivity. Plus they don't have to visit each supplier, but rather monitor and do it on an exception basis.

In fact, one customer put suppliers into three buckets: One we have to act on today, we know who to send and the magnitude. The second bucket was for those that have internal capacity and are important enough to us to move from midrange, but they aren't ready; send the right training material, so that the next month we can sit down and drive 20 percent cost savings. And the third bucket is not important enough to work with, or they don't have the processes to get there. Three groups—today to work on, work with tomorrow, and those we have to get rid of.

* * *

Allan Pinkham

Software is a great opportunity area. In decentralized companies sometimes one division will buy an application under a different contract for the same application that another plant is also buying for. It's a headache for the supplier, too. The solution is to combine all the different buys under one, with new terms and conditions, for a longer term agreement. You should be able to negotiate some savings—at least 20% or so—with the new agreement, so it's a win-win for everybody.

* * *

Steve Savignano, CEO
Ketera Technologies

Question:
In the past, three-five years, supply management investments in IT have taken on a new character. Many execs got
burned by casting projected ROIs for big systems, and the
benefits didn't develop. When you look out at industry now,
what do you see as the real mover that is causing companies
to consider your solution?
Answer:
In software, we've seen the opposite—something like,
"Here, let me sell you a Boeing 747, a runway and fleet of
trucks," and bingo, you are into project for 100M before you
can ship first $2 package! It's a sales model, a lot like a pyra-
mid scheme, but nobody will blow the whistle because they
are hoping to bring in one more person. Everyone questions
the fundamental economics of that model—gouging cash,
spending years to recapture value—and users are starting to
say sorry, that's not the way I do business. How does this
make sense? Let's look at the model again. You are spending
50-60% on sales and marketing in most software cos – why
is that? Well, the reason is that you have to do really good
marketing to sell the big packages!.
If you think about it, most business people in this space—
especially in the procurement space—make investment decisions all the time and want to know what the investment is
and what's the payback. That's why they are susceptible to
the ROI; the first rule of risk reduction is to look at how quickly
the payback comes. They are usually sold on a very large
ROI to justify large up front cash outlays.
We've taken a different approach. One of the things we
have tried to do is to say, look, this will cost you a reasonable
amount of money and you get a reasonable ROI. Let's work
on a model for quick investment, say 60-90 days, to get
going. This is what it costs to get started, here are the returns,
this looks good and you can put more investment in, but there
are checkpoints along the way. They can decide to commit

more, sort of like most things, they get to try to, get a feel for the value. That will happen more as people look at investments in business services, not big capital.

One example is ADP—payroll. That's compelling enough. In fact, there are huge parallels between spend management and payroll. So it's very important to do really well and on time. You don't get extra points, but if you don't do it, if people don't show up, you get no extra credit for doing it right, but the operations are very critical. The process is very complex, but strategically not of much value. We see customers look at all business processes, from the very complex and very critical to the not strategic—should be looking for supplier who is in business of aggregating, to build a solution to serve many customers. It doesn't make sense for businesses to do it themselves. There are no economies of scale. Investors will look at these and find things they have to do well but not necessarily themselves.

Here's another example. The average deal at SAP has dropped from $1M+ to 255K. People pay 100k, get value and tell SAP, I will fund next deal from savings from this deal. This is software model, trying to force itself into an on-demand model. One of the symptoms is that the deal size drops.

Another issue that goes along with the big software model is that, if I am a software co, and my customer pays 18% maintenance for updates, what is the opportunity to get revenue? It seems that the provider has to either give the customer more stuff or maintenance—more things so the customer will say okay. The whole issue with maintenance feels wrong: In the consumer world it's like getting tv —first buy an adapter for satellite tv whether you want it or not. What happens in the software world is that users use only 15% of the software stuff they buy. Business consumers end up with piles of stuff they don't use. Now the industry says, let's digest what I already have, and let's think about it before we sign on for another behemoth.

* * *

Brett Holland, COO
Akoya, Inc.
brett@akoyainc.com

When we look at cost savings, we know that 90% of it can be created in the design phase. But for most companies, the task of finding these opportunities can be overwhelming. It's hard to know where to begin with thousands of products and components that have accumulated over years and years of development.

Sometimes companies decide to outsource parts to China without actually knowing the true cost savings that these products could achieve and without giving engineers the opportunity to study and improve the cost of designs. We have a technology tool that takes product design data from a CAD file and runs it through a number of algorithms to identify possible cost savings. The application is called Akoya Cost Manageent Analytics (Akoya CMA), and the basis of the technology was developed by Caterpillar. Akoya CMA is commercially available as a web-enabled, on-demand tool. Basically the user dumps CAD files and some purchasing data into the machine and out pop gorgeous analytics displayed as graphics or neat charts looking at "should-costs" vs. market pricing or other costing approaches.

It's all part of moving the cost focus on analytics that allows buyers to truly understand their spend. Questions such as, "What would this design change do to total cost? " or "What does this group of items generally cost?" or "What would happen if we changed material specs?" are easily answered with good technology tools. Right now Akoya CMA is working on castings but will be analyzing other input materials using designs from various CAD file formats. Akoya estimates that it can cut 10% to 15% from the cost of castings just by looking closer at analytics.

The brain of the software is the modeling genius of Dr. Syamala Srinivasan and Nelson Jones of Caterpillar, with input from several of their top product engineers. Akoya has also incorporated feedback from some of the leading supply chain management organizations and biggest names in purchasing.

* * *

Blog Summary,
Transportation/Logistics/Packaging

Logistics represent nearly $1 trillion worth of costs every year, nearly 8.5% of the total U. S. Gross Domestic Product.

Dave Blanchard,
Logistics Today
January 2005, page 5

* * *

Allen@msg.com

If you are a big company, think about milk runs to save transportation money and build more consistency into your supply network. It probably won't work well if you are small company, because the objective is to make a series of stops and fill up the truck. In that case, consider buddying up—consolidating—with another small company with similar needs, and the two of you will save money. It worked for Toyota!

* * *

Rick Blasgen
Senior VP Integrated Logistics
ConAgra Foods, Inc.
rick.blasgen@conagrafoods.com

KEEP THAT DRIVER MOVING!
That's the biggest thing in transportation today. Capacity used to be viewed as near infinite, but now the market place is constrained. Carriers want to do business with "easier or friendly freight," i.e., easy delivery, easier pickups that don't tie up the driver, and no last-minute changes. Freeing up drivers'

time is paramount because of these constraints as well as hours of service regulations.

That means companies have to be very cognizant of transportation dollars they are spending and make those dollars more productive. Key is to get more sophisticated about carrier selection, volume commitments and reliability.

For example, consolidate to elevate order sizes. Here's an example. If yours is a multi-division company, are you shipping separate, and can you consolidate by going to the same customers or the same geographic area? By combining inventories into one location, you can begin to allow customers to combine items onto one order which is more efficient for all.

The other areas to watch in transportation include doing business with those providers who are reliable and provide electronic interchange. For example, when you tender a load to them, do they accept electronically ? Do they follow through on that commitment and provide status along the life cycle ? Do they then report once the shipment has been delivered in a timely way? These requirements are necessary if we are to be successful in understanding where inventory is along its journey.

You can obviously become more efficient if you eliminate bad information. If your supply chain is more reliable, and the carrier can count on the information, you're being a better partner. If transportation providers have access to accurate information earlier in the process, they can better manage their driver network, and reliability is improved.

Develop a detailed understanding of your negotiated rates with carriers. Help them to understand your volume and flows, giving them insight so they know when and where to position their equipment and drivers. This will improve the cost and reliability balance.

The whole idea is to keep the driver moving, make sure his or her downtime is minimum, and that the on-duty time is more efficient. For example, if a driver shows up but the distribution center is backed up for three hours, that's wasted driver time. So it's critical to understand how to make the receiving process more effective.

Another money-saving solution is the drop-trailer program. This program lets the driver come in, pick up a pre-loaded trailer and move on. Driver and driver retention are real cost factors, as well as quality of life issues. Over the long haul, schedules affect quality of life. Drivers say they would like to be home, so bad schedules cost industry drivers; and with the new restrictions, it becomes even more important for your company to meet schedule.

Everything we do is about satisfying the needs of customers and being more efficient. Collectively, we don't want drivers waiting. Work with the customer and design loads, solutions that make the whole process more efficient. Look at the type of pallets, the modules, how to configure the pallets, the load, to minimize hand stacking. Simply put, keep drivers driving.

* * *

Better logistics planning saves money. The factors that really drive transportation costs—distance and equipment utilization—are areas that few companies pay enough attention to outside of shipping departments.

Here's an example from a transplant. The Japanese love milk runs; they are complicated, but they work. An assembly plant had a complicated carpet delivery scheme for product coming from a supplier one hour away. The shipments had to be sequenced because there was not enough room at the installation point to display all the material. And the trigger point for sending the broadcast info to the carpet supplier didn't leave enough lead time to fill a truck.

Now, some companies would stop there and accept a less than perfect solution, but not this one. They wanted both the truck full and materials perfectly sequenced. It had to be perfectly on time, and the truck had to be fully utilized—the driver, tractor and trailer. And they figured it out with no computers! A supervisor planned it out step by step, drawing the process with a paper and pencil. They needed these carpets 8 times per day, to cover 2 shifts, every 2 hours. It only represented 2-3 racks of carpets, with lots of room left on the truck; so he set up what appeared to be a very complex route.

The truck would leave supplier A, go to windshield

manufacturing and fill up, then to the plant where it would get unloaded right away and then reloaded with the empty containers for the next route, which could be A or a different local route for full utilization. The next supplier would fill the empty containers, and then the truck would return to A to pick up the 3d shipment of the day and go to another supplier. The only way to do this was to draw it all out—it was all on kanban, and all the suppliers had to be on kanban, except for the carpet supplier that received a broadcast to color with a 4-hour lead time.

It was complicated because the plant was in an area with extremely unreliable traffic patterns, so they set up routes. Then they had the creator of the new schedule run the routes and actually physically stop at every place and look at the lead times to load and unload, etc. He ran the whole thing himself and developed all the patterns for each route. He even drew on graph paper how a truck should be configured.

The team provided the driver with point to point instructions—standard work! The whole process took about 3 or 4 weeks, including bringing in all the suppliers and the truckers and training them on the new process. They had to do it at different times to see the traffic patterns.

The first day of the new schedule was unforgettable. For the small trucker it was an all-new experience, but they had wanted a small company that was willing to learn. The first thing they did was to take all the drivers and show them exactly why: "We can only store this many carpets. If your truck is late, this line shuts down. We are relying on you to do perfectly."

There were six or seven different routes. Each driver drove the same route every day, so the drivers knew what they had to do; they would coach the people on the truck and would help load the truck, and they knew they had to get back on time— these were some very special drivers! On day one, the supervisor had to be there at 4 AM because the first run left before the shift. He worked 24 hours straight, right through the last run. On the 8th delivery from A, the team figured out they had a truck coming from the South every night and it went by A on the way, so there was room enough on the back for 2 racks. Every night the truck stopped at A, so they did not have to add another piece of equipment and another driver. It was a great way to learn certain techniques from actually doing them—kanban, standard work, visual controls, workplace org., pull.

* * *

Ken Ackerman
ken@warehousing-forum.com

My favorite, the most important technology breakthrough since bar coding came out 20 years ago, is voice recognition technology. I would focus on that. It's not the only thing, but it's the biggest. It's relatively modest to implement, works from the biggest to the smallest operations. You don't have to be a Wal-Mart to make this work. Much less complex and less costly. Kroger and Wal-Mart are now using it. VR saves 10-15% on order picking, and that's not the only place where you get the most dramatic savings.

* * *

Bob Silverman
President
Gross & Associates
Consultants in Material Handling Logistics
732-636-2666, rsilverman@grossassociates.com
www.grossassociates.com

The biggest expense category in most distribution centers is labor.

The distribution center job function with the most people is typically order picking.

Pickers spend more time traveling—whether walking or riding a vehicle, going up or down —than they spend doing everything else combined, including handling products, referring to paperwork, using a computer, scanning.

So if you're going to do one specific thing in your distribution center to reduce your costs, I'd recommend attacking order pickers' travel.

There are a number of ways to do this:

One is to create a forward pick zone—a warehouse within a warehouse, used for order picking. Items are replenished to this area from reserve storage. It does result in an additional handling function (replenishment), but usually the picking labor savings far outweigh the replenishment labor.

Forward pick lines can be made far more productive by slotting the items in them by movement. Pareto's 80/20 rule generally holds true—20 percent of the items will result in 80 percent of the picking activity. By putting these fastest movers in a concentrated area, travel distances can be greatly reduced for most of your orders.

Improved material handling equipment can make picking more efficient.

Double pallet jacks instead of standard jacks for picking full case orders

Carton flow racks, to increase pick position density and separate pickers from replenishers, reducing congestion.

Carousel and automated storage/retrieval systems to bring the product to the picker.

When properly applied, these systems can triple or quadruple pick productivity by all by eliminating travel—the products come to the picker automatically. But beware — you have to carefully analyze your order data to ensure they're a good fit.

Other ways to save money within a distribution center include:

Using a Warehouse Management System (WMS) to control the distribution operation. A WMS controls the movement and storage of materials within an operation and processes for the associated transactions, such as receiving, putaway, replenishment, picking, packing, and shipping. It also manages the inventory and item locations, controls and optimizes warehouse labor, and has interfaces for automation and equipment.

Reduce space requirements by:

Using lift trucks that require narrower aisles

Fully utilizing the facility clear height (maximizing cube utilization)

Storing in depth to reduce the number of aisles

Using multiple height pallet rack openings

Using different storage modules for different products instead of a "one solution fits all" approach

Eliminating obsolete inventory

Optimizing pallet patterns

Transportation costs can be reduced by using better pallet patterns and using cube optimization software to improve truck loading. Look at drop shipping items from your vendor to your customer to reduce both the labor involved in handling the item and the associated transportation costs.

Better information is generally the key to reducing overall logistics and supply chain costs. There are dozens of examples, a simple one being that knowing what's on a truck before it arrives in your facility can allow you to better prepare for how you're going handle unloading it, reducing labor and space requirements.

* * *

Mark Richards
Vice President
Associated Warehouses, Inc.
714.538.5990
Mark@AWILogistics.com
Pres., Council of Supply Chain Management
Professionals

You want to preserve capital, which you're putting into systems and buildings, for things with a higher return, such as marketing, new manufacturing technology and R & D.

Another approach for small to medium sized companies is to outsource your supply chain requirements and consolidate your business with compatible product going to the same customer or similar geographic area. This enables you to reduce transportation costs. Instead of shipping via more expensive LTL your product can ship at full truck rates, allowing you to easily save 20% plus. Also you will preserve capital when outsourcing because the 3rd party will have the scale to invest in the best technology, such as execution software. Example: One of the people we work with is in the pre-audit and payment business. This company has advanced systems that enable them to efficiently receive invoice detail from carriers. They take this information, compare it with what they know the shipper and mfg had agreed to, confirm that the invoice is accurate and then enter the information into the system. When it's entered in the system, the manufacturer can have visibility of the shipment. This also allows the 3PL to provide the shippers with an easy to use tool that enables them to identify the low cost carrier for each shipment. This is very valuable, as you will often have people, when they are in the heat of the battle, calling "Joe Premium Carrier" when there might be a better way. But without tools, if you don't have the expertise it's very challenging.

With some software it doesn't have to be expensive. This is subscription-based, Terminal Server Technology, in the $400 per month range, from a company called The Logistics Department in Orange, California, called their Rate Shopper product. The point is you don't have to spend a lot of money because it's hosted on a service, and you don't have to invest in additional technolgy. Investing in it yourself would be very challenging to capture rate data, organize it and have system do the product, weight. It looks at 30 different carriers and makes recommendations. The process gives people visibility for making better decisions. You don't even need the transportation manager. Anyone with even minimal computer skills can arrange for a shipment. They simply go to the system, enter a few pieces of information such as destination, Zip and the weight of the shipment, and the RateShop software identifies the optimum decision. The system can even send an e-mail to the carrier to let them know it's ready, and they give confirmation.

You are empowering the people at the dock to make quality decisions; they are more engaged in the process. At the same time, if you do have a shipping event, the system logs and tracks it, so periodically someone in the organization can see if they are taking advantage of the best way, instead of just using your "favorite" carrier.

Other suggestion: Another thing you can do is to work on collaboration. The Aberdeen Group talked about what supply chain leaders are doing differently. Their findings were alarming, and they show the value of collaborations. Buyers and planners use 1/3 to 1/2 of their time to resolve disruptions; 40 percent of managers resolve last minute issues based on habit and gut feel. That's where execution software comes in. Companies that employ technologies to minimize cost and the frequency of disruptions have significantly higher fill rates and improved customer service

* * *

INTEGRATED PACKAGING SYSTEMS, INC.
David Bartylla, President
(208) 345-9312 Office
(208) 867-2853 Cellular
davidb@intpkgsys.com

How to save money in packaging
Three key areas immediately come to mind: line control, accumulation and case packing. Most are overlooked to varying degrees, depending on the size of company and the internal resources available.

Line Control—Lines tend to start and stop haphazardly. That costs money, in terms of downtime. It causes damage and holds up other operations. By incorporating more line controls, it is possible to stop and start the line in a more controlled manner. With further enunciation, the operator can respond quicker to stoppages and more easily identify what the cause of the problem is.

Accumulation—Imagine a packaging line which sends bottles down a conveyor to an automatic labeling machine, with an in-line, first-in/first-out accumulation system (i.e., the simplistic equivalent of a table off to the side as a buffer zone) for when the labeler jams. Strategic points of accumulation within packaging line designs, such as this, compensate for a period of machine downtime and other interruptions. In many instances, it actually prevents shutting down a line, in this case the filler; which can be expensive and generate low and high fill levels in the process. Thus, a moneysaving tip is to strategically incorporate accumulation into your line design, with line control, to effectively reduce downtime or increase uptime.

Case Packing—People don't always focus on case packing, but it is so important for logistics costs. It's vital to plan the secondary and tertiary packaging, as well as other associated product cost contributors. Ask questions. How do I use the volume on the pallet, in the case, or around the container, as efficiently as possible? Can we reduce distribution costs by more optimally loading the shipping trailer in terms of a more efficient pallet cube, case cube, etc.? Is there a better way? And more importantly, is this better way still easy to apply with quick line changeovers and product flexibility in mind?

Another possible savings area is packaging materials. There is a tendency to overspecify materials, which adds to product costs. For example, we have a client that was using a particular five-layer film to suit certain shelf-life requirements. The material was thick, stiff and quite expensive. By reevaluating the needs and working closely with different film suppliers, it was determined that a three-layer film could match quality and provide substantial savings.

Many people think a box is a box. Companies don't always go through the analysis to consider wall thickness and compression strength. And of course the box seller is in business to sell fiber; with competition forcing many material reduction considerations along the way. Larger companies have internal resources to compare the trade-offs and reach the best solutions. Corrugated strength relative to stacking methods on the pallet and further stacking strength from internal primary package integrity can be of great consequence. Many times, the case design can be changed and/or the corrugated board weight can be reduced, which further provides savings.

Although many smaller companies don't have resources dedicated to enhancing the packaging lines and associated materials on a proactive and ongoing basis, they can still save money by taking a close look at the details. There is a significant range of equipment, equipment features or options, line designs, packages, and associated materials to consider. There are specialists out there who are focused on these issues ... day in and day out. They've seen various solutions in hundreds of different plants. Even though the conditions may be similar, in all truth they're never the same, particularly with changing technologies.

A smaller company can save millions by selecting good equipment, focusing on a solid line design with control and accumulation, reducing line downtime and being smart about their packaging materials. Remember ... unless you challenge the current approach, you're probably missing a good savings opportunity. It's clearly worth the effort.

* * *

10 percent savings in packaging at least!

Packaging impacts quality, costs and even timing of ship schedules. Be sure that your packaging representative from purchasing or design sits on the new product team because they can save you money on both inbound and outbound shipments. The information that the team requires includes detail about the new product, including finish, weight and other cosmetic features. The team will want to calculate some starting number of returnable containers to figure that into the overall cost projections. The same time the design engineers are finalizing the product, the packaging people need to design and test prototypes and samples to evaluate different solutions and their costs. The idea is to wade through all the possible packaging solutions in advance of product launch, considering shipping options around space and loads, as well as inbound unpack and production issues. The companies that do packaging planning the best have good relationships with a limited number of suppliers. They know how to optimize filling containers, and they work hard at planning the utilization of shipping space. There is lots of opportunity at many stages of the whole cycle to optimize cost savings and to protect quality, another cost factor, as well. It's not just about looking for better freight rates or locating a good trucker. That's where software is a good investment, because the tradeoffs and the financial considerations, once you get into this, are huge. You can easily save 10 percent just by studying returnable packaging and how the product fills the container.

* * *

cthompson@ups.com
Chad Thompson, CPP, CPLP
Corporate Packaging Manager
UPS Professional Services
Phn: 630-628-3710, Fax: 630-628-3727

Damage Control: Package integrity starts with the shipper.
 We work with the customer to optimize their packaging, reduce damages and lower costs, all of which help increase customer satisfaction and loyalty and improve on-time delivery. So our focus is on reducing or preventing damage and second, what to do to minimize cost of packaging and transportation. Those are key driving factors for our engagement with customers.

With the UPS small parcel environment, 13.6 million packages/day go through the system. Imagine the diversity of products moving through the network.

Worldwide we have over 1,700 operating centers across the world. UPS operates on a hub and spoke network. Each of these centers is geographically linked, so we can provide timely and reliable service to every address. We carry packages up to 150 pounds and relatively large—165 inches of length and girth—small nuts and bolts, equipment, furniture, etc. We cover incredible diversity. So we do approach each customer on a case by case basis. We have clients every day looking for packaging solutions, and our goal is to provide them with customized solutions to meet their specific needs.

Examples: I worked with a company, the leading fastener manufacturer—metal and plastic used in small parts in wide variety of industries. They were experiencing a high incidence of product loss problems—loose parts breaking out of cartons ripping open and product scattering. They were losing product in transit, and packages were being delivered with shortages. For instance, if the customer ordered 1,000, they would get 800. The problem created lots of reshipments and customer dissatisfaction.

When they came to us, they wanted better packaging to optimize containment and protection. We took their products, looked at the problem, evaluated and tested, and redesigned the packaging in a our laboratory, then validated the performance of the new packaging using industry developed and approved test standards. The new design looked the same, but it did reduce the cube of the package to make it more dense, not so loose and flowing. For the new package, we also changed material properties, with better tear resistance, but this did not raise the cost of material. Actually, we reduced the amount of material they needed because of cube, so the client saw significant improvement.

A China example: We recently did the packaging design for a furniture company producing in China. Coming in from China, the biggest thing is the space utilization of containers. We don't want to ship air, we want to make it as dense as possible. Back to my original questions, working with customers to reduce their damages and package costs involves two steps:

1. We will always, most important, use package performance testing standards to develop the most appropriate and cost effective packaging solution. Several shipping companies don't give much thought to packaging. It's an afterthought. They focus on product and not packaging, often resulting in high risk exposure to product damage. Or they put too much packaging into it, spending much more than they need to. Our function at UPS Professional Services is to use the most current laboratory testing standards that accurately simulates the real-world distribution environment, so we can accurately evaluate and assess the product protection performance of the packaging. We have a lab in Addison, Illinois, a relatively high tech lab, where we have all the different types of testing capabilities to simulate handling and transport conditions such as shock, vibration, compression and atmospheric.

This is where the advance in testing has come a long way. I sit on boards of testing associations that develop testing procedures, to simulate as accurately as possible the normal handling conditions. You don't want to test for the abnormal, you don't want to over-package. That's where performance testing will ensure your package will get the best protection for least cost.

All the staff at our UPS Test lab are degreed packaging engineers.

How to pick where to start? Start with the most help-needed products, the ones experiencing higher frequency of damages, and frequency is the key area to look at. If you have 50 of one product getting damage and 25 of another, the common response is, "Let's attack the 50." But that might be the wrong one. Look at percentage of damages to percentage of items shipped where you can target more appropriately for greatest impact. Try for small changes in packaging, small cost increases, if any.

Focus in on areas where most help is needed.

Sometimes we get customers looking at product they want to address because transportation costs are too high, not just packaging. We had a client in the last 5-6 weeks. They had a very good package, no damages, but transportation costs were so high because of cube and size of the package. They were spending a lot of money on air. The shipments were coming from Mexico into a distribution center, then broken down—we're talking electronics — where in the US it ships out as single packages to the consumer by UPS. So the full truckload from Mexico is the problem. We estimate we can take 5 daily truckloads down to 3-4 per day, will save money with more efficient package, so we will scale down the packaging to the minimum without compromising product protection. We'll get 15 – 20 percent savings.

* * *

Returnable packing

You've heard the phrase, "Cardboard is not a world class material!" Have suppliers use plastic totes for transporting inside the plant. Cardboard is expensive, and it is the number one cause of dust and some quality issues, in plants. The initial investment for plastic will pay for itself.

The principles of lean manufacturing apply to save money in logistics—milk runs, maintaining a full truck on a regular basis, keeping high truck utilization and still have small LTLs by sharing across divisions and regions. If your company is decentralized, it will be harder to do this, because the first requirement is data aggregation with all info about the product, weight, cube, pallet requirements, etc.

With China it's even more important to look at total cost because leadtimes and shipping choices have all changed. You can't do it on a blackboard anymore!

Construct a network model and try some scenarios with different locations and providers. Spreadsheets are not so good because they are not flexible. You want to actually see the simulation, be able to compare tradeoffs. Savings estimate: 5-15% on logistics costs.

On perishables, position fastest moving SKUs closest to the shipping dock.

* * *

Blog Summary, Benefits

Jane Edlund, janeedlund@yahoo.com

Health care Costs—Wellness Saves Money
Self-insurance, exercise and diet, ergonomically correct work, 7 steps to wellness.

I have an exercise background and can help people with exercise that works with their lifestyle. I work for the Wellness Center at the U. of Montana, and my job is to help employees fit exercise into their workweek. Some people are willing to join a gym, some want simple program at home, some people want me to come to their office and do exercises with them. We have gone to 6 different departments at the university. They find me a little room, and they bring an exercise mat or a towel. We do core body abs—all muscles involved with posture—and then breathing and relaxation. Sometimes it's over coffee breaks, but 30 minutes is ideal. I train people from 13 to 90, the oldest, with the whole gamut of weaknesses, from diabetes, osteoporosis, to hip and knee replacements.

Once they do it, the very first thing they notice is they have so much more energy, and they sleep better—in the first two weeks!. Then it becomes a mental thing —they feel more in control of their life, they feel stronger and they start to feel more confident.

If they don't do it, it's a downward spiral—they're tired all the time, they eat poorly, don't sleep well, have no energy and their work suffers.

* * *

233

Hughes Electronics offering a disease-management program to its 7,000 employees, since 1998 " . . . consistently produced an almost 3:1 return on investment."
—Pamela Hymel, vice president of human resources, *Workforce Management,* "More Care, Less Cost," March 2004, pp. 55-58

The plan includes voluntary health-risk assessment and wellness component focused on prevention. Costs average $5-12 per year per employee/per condition.
—Watson Wyatt, ibid.

Briggs and Stratton in-house health clinic, opened in 2003, saved $500,000 in costs. "There's only one way to avoid paying more and more for the health-care system," says Shiely, Briggs's chief executive, "and that's for corporations to get back into the health-care business."
—"A Cure for High Health costs: In-house Company Clinics," Vanessa Fuhrmans, *Wall Street Journal,* Feb. 11, 2005

Self-insurance, self-funded company health plans save money. Self-insurance is the method in which companies pay for their employees' medical expenses. The company hires a third-party administrator to manage its healthcare, but pays it own bill. If employee medical expenses rise, so does company liability. If employees stay healthy, the company and employees, who usually pay a portion of the expenses, save. So it pays to stay healthy! "The savings can be fairly substantial, from ten percent to 20 percent of their normal premium," says William Breidenbach, president of Health Plans Inc., a company that specializes in administering self-funded plans.
—"Weighing health coverage options: Self-insurance on the rise," Andy Murray, *Gloucester Daily Times Online,* March 17, 2005

If you have several thousand employees, self-funding is the way to control health care costs. Because statistically 20 percent of the population uses 80 percent of health care dollars. How can the employer save ten percent? If you have a company that is currently fully insured, on a cycle of rates going up and benefits going down, look at the rates, decide what kind of benefit you want to provide and if you want to take on some of the risk.

A Wellness program at Highsmith, a Wisconsin marketer of supplies and equipment to schools and libraries, lowered their costs; premiums rose only 3.1 percent in 2003, and 2.9 percent in 2002

Turnover has slowed to 8.7 percent

"Workers' compensation costs haven't just slowed down, they've actually gone down . . . [to an amount] significantly less than what we were paying in the early '90s," according to Bill Herman, Highsmith vice president for human resources.

—quoted in "Wellness on the Bottom Line," Philip Harper, *Microsoft Small Business Center On-line* newsletter, February, 2005

* * *

Appendix

cmoody1@ford.com
Chad Moody
Ford Motor Company
Cost Optimization

Subject: "Design Change Friendly" Supplier Quote Cost Breakdown Worksheets

Competitive bidding typically drives lower up-front supplier prices when the sourcing carrot is dangled in front of them, so many suppliers try to "make back their money" on design changes after they have been locked. And, at least in the auto industry, post-sourcing design changes during the product development process and even after mass production can be a huge cost driver. Many companies don't have either the time or a very good method of analyzing design change costs.

This cost savings idea is to provide a worksheet that easily enables analysis of design change costs. The worksheet provided is an example of my own creation. We don't "officially" use this currently at Ford. Honda did use something along these lines. I had great success with it there.

Here's how to decipher the fictional (but based on factual previous experiences) story found in the spreadsheet:

The spreadsheet worksheet named "Typical Supplier Quote Cost Breakdown Worksheet" shows a commonly-used quote breakdown for a part that has undergone a design change from a Revision Level 1 to a Revision Level 2. The supplier was already sourced the business at $1.98 through a competitive bidding process at the Revision Level 1. You can see the selling price of the part after the design change to Revision Level 2 jumped to $2.30. Even though the supplier provided a cost breakdown of the $2.30 price, how can we tell if this is a good number? The supplier has been sourced, so we can't use another round of time-consuming competitive bidding to verify cost competitiveness. The answer is to require the supplier to provide a quote breakdown in a format like the ones found on the two spreadsheet worksheets on pages 243 and 244 of this Appendix.

The new and improved quote breakdown on these spreadsheets requires the supplier to perform a clear cost walk from the old design to the new design. It leaves little room for suppliers to hide fat in their design change costs since everything that has changed is clearly indicated. This enables a quick review of what happened in the change, and suggests questions like those shown on the 1st of the two recommended work-sheets. Once the supplier is challenged to justify their costs by these questions, positive results thru a re-quote usually occur, like the results shown on the 2nd of the two recommended worksheets named "After Analysis." It causes the design change costs to be resolved easily in a fact-based manner, which should provide a fair solution to both the customer and suppli-er. And, being that there is now less opportunity to hide fat in their costs, suppliers will be less likely to attempt to do so on future changes.

This type of breakdown sheet can also be used to ana-lyze new model part costing as well. I recall using this type of methodology on the new model 1998 Honda Accord. As I recall, during the early product develop-ment stages and before sourcing the 1998 Accord Lighting parts, we asked suppliers to develop design ideas to take 30% out of the price of the current parts. The goal was to help understand the design competi-tiveness of the suppliers to help us in the supplier selection process. We required the use of these types of sheets for their responses, so we could easily see both the design and cost walk between the current part and a new model proposal. As you probably know, there is usually cost creep between the "Job Last" price of a part phasing out of production, and the "Job 1st" price of the new model design replacing it. This type of spread-sheet can help control this.

The nice thing about this breakdown worksheet is that it can be developed and up and running in a matter of hours. It takes virtually no investment, yet the payback can be huge.

* * *

Example spreadsheets follow . . .

Typical Supplier Quote Breakdown Worksheet

Part Number	123456
Part Design Level	Revision Level 2
Part Name	Applique Assembly

Raw Material	Lbs		Cost/Lb		Total	
Polypropylene Resin	0.8000	$	0.51	$	0.41	
1010 Steel	0.2500	$	0.30		0.08	
					-	
					-	
				$	0.48	

Purchased Parts	Qty		Cost/Unit		Total	
Screw	5	$	0.03	$	0.15	
Clip	5	$	0.05		0.25	
					-	
					-	
				$	0.40	

Labor	Minutes		Cost/Min		Total	
Mold Resin Applique	0.8750	$	0.43	$	0.38	
Stamp Steel Bracket	0.0200	$	0.43		0.01	
					-	
					-	
				$	0.38	

Burden	Minutes		Cost/Min		Total	
Mold Resin Applique	0.8750	$	0.59	$	0.52	
Stamp Steel Bracket	0.0200	$	0.72		0.01	
					-	
					-	
				$	0.53	

SG&A and Profit		% of Mfg Cost	Total	
Markup on Mfg Cost		15.2	$	0.27

Engineering	Total Cost		Part Life Volume	Total	
Design/Testing Services	$	143,000	800,000	$	0.18

Packaging	Parts/Container		Cost/Container		Total	
Returnable Tote	16	$	-	$	-	
3 Part Dividers	16	$	0.85		0.05	
				$	0.05	

Total Quoted Part Price		$	2.30

The price a
the previou
design leve
was $1.98
How can
analyze wh
caused th
jump to $2.3

Previous quoted price

Raw Material	Lbs	Cost/Lb	Total
Polypropylene Res	0.6500	$ .51	0.33
1010 Steel	0.2500	$ .30	0.06
		$	0.41

Purchased Parts	Qty	Cost/Unit	Total
Screw	5	$ 0.03	0.15
Clip	4	$ 0.05	0.20
		$	0.35

Labor	Minutes	Cost/min	Total
Mold resin applique	0.7500	$ 0.43	0.32
Stamp steel bracket	0.0200	$ 0.43	0.01
		$	0.33

Burden	Minutes	Cost/min	Total
Mold resin applique	0.7500	$ 0.59	0.44
Stamp steel bracket	0.0200	$ 0.72	0.01
		$	0.46

SG&A & Profit	% mfg costs		Total
Mark up on mfg cost	15.2		0.23

Engineering	Total Cost	Part life vol.	Total
Design/test	$ 125,000	800,000	0.16

Packaging	Parts/container		Total
Returnable tote	20	$	--
3 part dividers	20	$ 0.85	0.04
		$	0.04

Total Previous Part Price	$	1.98

Changes

Raw Material	Lbs	Cost/Lb	Change/Amt
Polypropylene Res	0.1500	$ 0.51	0.08

Did the part really grow this much?

Purchased Parts	Qty	Cost/Unit	Total
Clip	1	$ 0.05	0.05
		$	0.05

Labor	Minutes	Cost/min	Total
Mold resin applique	0.1250	$ 0.43	0.05
		$	0.05

Should molding cycle time really increase so much?

Burden	Minutes	Cost/min	Total
Mold resin applique	0.1250	$ 0.59	0.07
		$	0.07

SG&A & Profit	% mfg costs		Total
Mark up on mfg cost	15.2		0.07

Engineering	Total Cost	Part life vol.	Total
Design/test	$ 18,000	800,000	0.02

Did it really take this long to update the design?

Why are there fewer parts in a box?

Packaging	Parts/container		Total
3 part dividers	-4	$ 0.85	0.01
		$	0.01

Total Price Change	$	0.33

New Price

Raw Material	
$	0.41
	0.08
$	0.48

Purchased Parts	
$	0.15
	0.25
$	0.40

Labor	
$	0.38
	0.01
$	0.38

Burden	
$	0.52
	0.01
$	0.53

SG&A & Profit	
$	0.27

Engineering	
$	0.18

Packaging	
$	-
	0.05
	0.05

$	2.30

Breakdown for Revised Quote, Level 2

Previsous quoted price

Raw Material	Lbs	Cost/Lb	Total
Polypropylene Res	0.6500	$ .51	0.33
1010 Steel	0.2500	$ .30	0.06
			$ 0.41

Purchased Parts	Qty	Cost/Unit	Total
Screw	5	$ 0.03	0.15
Clip	4	$ 0.05	0.20
			$ 0.35

Labor	Minutes	Cost/min	Total
Mold resin applique	0.7500	$ 0.43	0.32
Stamp steel bracket	0.0200	$ 0.43	0.01
			$ 0.33

Burden	Minutes	Cost/min	Total
Mold resin applique	0.7500	$ 0.59	0.44
Stamp steel bracket	0.0200	$ 0.72	0.01
			$ 0.46

SG&A & Profit	% mfg costs	Total
Mark up on mfg cost	15.2	0.23

Engineering	Total Cost	Part life vol.	Total
Design/test	$ 125,000	800,000	0.16

Packaging	Parts/container		Total
Returnable tote	20	$	--
3 part dividers	20	$ 0.85	0.04
			$ 0.04

Total Previous Part Price	$ 1.98

Changes

Raw Material	Lbs	Cost/Lb	Change/Amt
Polypropylene Res	0.0200	$ 0.51	0.01
			$ 0.01

Purchased Parts	Qty	Cost/Unit	Total
Clip	1	$ 0.05	0.05
			$ 0.05

Labor	Minutes	Cost/min	Total
Mold resin applique	0.0100	$ 0.43	0.00
			$ 0.00

Burden	Minutes	Cost/min	Total
Mold resin applique	0.0100	$ 0.59	0.01
			$ 0.01

SG&A & Profit	% mfg costs	Total
Mark up on mfg cost	15.2	0.01

Engineering	Total Cost	Part life vol.	Total
Design/test	$ 1,000	800,000	0.00

Packaging	Parts/container		Total
3 part dividers	0	$ 0.85	----
			$ ----

Total Price Change	$ 0.08

New Price

Raw Material	
$	0.34
	0.08
$	0.42

Purchaseed Parts	
$	0.15
	0.25
$	0.40

Labor	
$	0.33
	0.00
$	0.34

Burden	
$	0.45
	0.01
$	0.46

SG&A & Profit	
$	0.25

Engineering	
$	0.16

Packaging	
$	-
	0.04
	0.04

$	2.06

For further reading

Billion Dollar Turnaround, William T. Monahan, Oaklea Press, Richmond, Virginia, 2005

Breakthrough Partnering, Patricia E. Moody, John Wiley and Sons, New York, 1993

The Incredible Payback, Dave Nelson, Patricia E. Moody and Jonathan R. Stegner, Amacom, New York City, 2005

The Kaizen Blitz, Anthony C. Laraia, Patricia E. Moody and Robert W. Hall, John Wiley and Sons, New York, 1999

Lean Transformation, Bruce A. Henderson, Jorge L Largo, Oaklea Press, Richmond, Virginia, 1999

Powered by Honda, Dave Nelson, Rich Mayo and Patricia E. Moody, John Wiley and Sons, New York, 1998

Product Development for the Lean Enterprise, Mike Kennedy, Oaklea Press, Richmond, Virginia, 2003

The Purchasing Machine, How the Top Ten Companies Use Best Practices to Manage Their Supply Chains, Patricia E. Moody, The Free Press, Simon and Schuster, New York, 2001

PATRICIA E. MOODY,CMC

Patricia E. Moody is a seasoned, non-traditional operations guru. Direct and outspoken, relentless and extremely focused on balanced results, she is trusted to provide C-level executives the kind of counsel they rely on to generate real success. She likes to compete and win, and she expects her clients to do the same.

Ms. Moody has some 12 books to her credit. She was named by *Fortune* magazine one of the Ten Pioneering Women in Manufacturing, she was featured on CNN's "21ST CENTURY WITH BERNARD SHAW, broadcast to 16 million people worldwide. She has an MBA and an Honorary Doctorate, and she is certified by the Institute of Management Consultants. Her client list includes Motorola, Respironics, British Petroleum, Waste Management, Cisco, Her industry experience includes driving a fork-truck - not well - and consulting to Johnson & Johnson's McNeil Consumer Labs during the Tylenol poisoning crisis; she is credited with saving the company.

A pragmatic visionary and self-confessed technology freak, she has little patience for laggards who have dwelled too long seeking one-note methodologies. She believes that a combination of technology, clear process, and progressive leadership, funded by smart spend management, can save endangered companies.

Ms. Moody welcomes your correspondance - write to her and her team, Blon --- er, Brenda Soufflet, Sean Bittbeiter, and the rest of the characters of United Manufacturing, at tricia@PatriciaEMoody.com. Make it brief. Or visit http://www.PatriciaEMoody.com.